THE SOUL *in* GRIEF

THE SOUL *in* GRIEF

Love, Death and Transformation

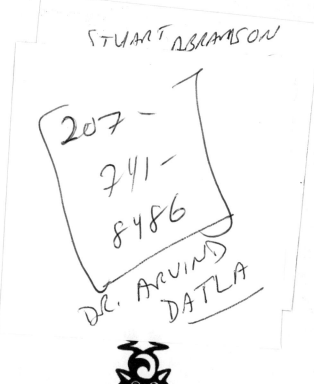

Frog Ltd.
Berkeley, California

The Soul in Grief: love, death and transformation

Published by Frog, Ltd.

Frog, Ltd. books are distributed by
North Atlantic Books
P.O. Box 12327
Berkeley, CA 94712

Cover art by Stephen Quiller
Cover design by Ayelet Maida
Book Design by Joan Stepp Smith

Printed in the United States of America

Distributed to the book trade by Publishers Group West

Library of Congress Cataloging-in Publication Data

Romanyshyn, Robert D. (Robert Donald), 1942 -
 The soul in grief: love, death and transformation /
Robert D. Romanyshyn.
     p.   cm.
     ISBN 1-55643-315-8 (alk. paper)
     1. Grief. 2. Bereavement—Psychological aspects. 3. Death—
Psychological aspects. 4. Jungian psychology.
     I. Title.
BF575.G7 R65 1999
155.9' 37—dc21   99-29798
                                                                          CIP

CONTENTS

PART THREE ~ LYRICAL IMPROVISATIONS IN CELEBRATION OF THE WORLD

DEDICATION

Janet

1946 – 1992

Your loving smile now the radiance of a Star,

Your generous spirit now the bounty of the Sea:

You opened my heart to love and I made you laugh.

ACKNOWLEDGMENTS

An expansion of the soul's capacity to love can be the gift of grief endured. This book charts that journey of transformation. I want to acknowledge here my sons, Jeffrey and Andrew, who suffered the work of grief in their own ways, and who supported me in my own grieving.

I also wish to acknowledge the many friends who walked with me. They know who they are and that I hold them in my heart as I write these words. A very special acknowledgement goes to Charles Asher, who, in the darkest hour, performed a most difficult and courageous act for me. I will never forget.

Finally, I want to acknowledge Veronica. From the hills of Devon, England, through the wilds of the bush in South Africa and all the places in between—the starry night skies of Venasque, France, the tranquil hills of Tuscan, Italy, and the magical pyramids of Teotihuacan in Mexico—she has been my loving spouse and faithful companion. Without her this book could not have been written. Love experienced once in a lifetime is a treasure. Twice is a miracle. Thank you for the miracle.

FOREWORD

This is a beautifully musty book. As I read it, my imagination was visited by memories of quiet summer monastery lanes, where I walked in retreat falling ever more deeply into questions about my future and the demands of my passions—and I was only eighteen. I re-sense the smoky fragrance of the single malt scotch whiskey they make on the island of Skye, a drink my good Celtic friends always brought out at the end of a discussion on the soul, a drink my wife will only sniff because its aroma gives her everything she wants from it. I'm reminded of Proust and the singular insight that as we breathe in the subtle wafts of the world around us, we begin to become aware and to imagine. I feel comforted in becoming reacquainted with the value of melancholy, a humor that has never been far from my sensation. The book seems to me to be about the counterpoint of reverie and melancholy.

I'm reminded of a moment two years ago, on a rare visit to his part of California, when I happened to pass Robert on a stone walk a few yards from his study, noticing immediately the ashen shade of his mourning. It thrills me to see that pale face and those pained eyes transformed and redeemed in these beautiful pages. I'm also delighted to see, in Robert's capable hands, psychology itself moving into language that is neither poetry nor science nor philosophy. This is phenomenology in only the most refined sense, a delicate cusping of sense impression and interior imagination and the creation of a third place between person and environs. I have long sought a way of using words that would take us authors and readers onto a plane that hovers between things and experience without taking away from either. Robert is achieving this, and I expect this pivotal book to be the beginning of a fruitful style not only for him but for anyone wishing to be released from the hard prison of literal speech and untethered abstraction.

How important our mourning is, and how blind our ways of desperately seeking distance from our melancholy! Americans run for the nearest and steadiest sunshine, not only in their search for a geographical home, but for an emotional safety zone. If this book would do nothing more than portray the beauty proper to melancholy, it would be a valuable resource. But it does more, connecting sadness to a particular way of imagining—reverie. Play Claude Debussy's piano piece *Reverie* as background to these words, as I have done, and notice that your imagination has a clear geography, the music and language truly transporting you to a special place having its own emotional tone and its placing of meaning. The instrument is the message. The writer's carefully conjured words spirit us in this geography and not their meaning alone.

Psychology disappears in the language of sheer facts and personality dynamics and structures. It also disappears in a reaction against the interior life as it chases into the world as a psychology of things. The secret of being psychological is to leave this Newtonian world altogether and speak from a place of intense sensation, impression, and reverie. This book is appropriately a reverie on reverie, a melancholic monologue on melancholy. All of these confluences lead me to trust it, and it is never easy to trust psychology, a discipline that seems hell bent on pursuing veiled moralisms rather than evoking bodily wisdom.

So, forget psychology as the scientific study of human behavior or as the analysis of the psyche or even as an interpretation of the world. Forget self-help and the helping professions. Forget all helping. Forget psychology as a field or discipline. Forget psychologizing yourself. Forget psychology.

Robert is introducing us to a new way of imagination that has direct relevance to our everyday situation, especially to its strong emotions and its scarcity of meaning, and yet is completely without normative guidance and normative description. I would think it is a form of education of the deepest sort, the kind that happens when we are forced to find a way to live in the midst of grief. If there is any one thing our culture needs in this time of decadence, it is true education, a forming of self and soul, society and place, emotion and meaning.

Enter this musty world as you would look at old photographs of your family and friends. I don't think the mind alone will sense the place as friendly, but the soul will feel completely at home. Don't try to understand, but do try to accept all the many invitations presented here for reverie and reflection. This is not a book of information; it is a book of emotional and imaginal places. It demands an intimacy of reading that may seem unusual and challenging, but that intimacy is part of its message. Ultimately, as any work of art would be that is concentrated on the soul, it is a book about love.

THOMAS MOORE
JANUARY 1997

PART ONE

A JOURNEY WITHOUT MAPS

In the middle of the journey of our life
I came to my senses in a dark forest,
for I had lost the straight path.

~ Dante Alighieri

CHAPTER

1

Songs of a Gypsy

REVERIES ~

AWAKENING FROM SLEEP

Each day brought with it a renewal of that leaden heaviness of grief. Nights spent in aimless wandering, consciousness dimmed by wine, the morning, each morning and its light, was an agony. By midday the body, not the I who could choose or make decisions, would collapse, and through sheer exhaustion I would fall into sleep. It was during one of those afternoon falls that something like a miracle happened.

The sound echoed through the house; on the edge of consciousness, I could hardly imagine its cause. Heavy with sleep, I tried to ignore what had awakened me, but curiosity, and a little fear urged me from my bed. Finding nothing disturbed in my bedroom, I walked through the house, but each room only mirrored the same sleepy deadness I felt within my own soul. Everything in these rooms was cold and far away, and between me and these things there was no spirit of love, no warmth, no spark of animation, no connection. They were alien things and I an alien, a stranger, amongst them.

The last room was my den: a desk, a chair, and a wall of bookshelves. It was to be a place for writing, but in the six months that I had been there not a word had been written at the desk. In fact, the room was hardly ever entered and was, perhaps, the coldest of all. In quickly scanning it, however, I discovered the origin of the noise that had awakened me. In the far end corner, some shelves of a bookcase had collapsed. I knew even before I approached it that it was the shelves containing the books and the articles that I had written and published over the course of some twenty years. Of the three shelves in this room, all identical, it was this one which had fallen. Of all the bookshelves in the house, it was this one, the one holding my life, which had collapsed.

Weary and despondent, I hardly cared. I was only angry at the mess and at the work it would take to repair the shelves and to replace the books. But from some ancient sense of duty, rather than with any sense of love, I did so, replacing and arranging the books as they had been before, according to the years of their publication. Satisfied, I left the room and returned to sleep.

Three days later I was awakened again by the same noise. Returning to the room I sat amidst the fallen books. This time, however, something else took hold of me, and in place of anger and despair, I felt some curiosity. A year earlier my life had collapsed with the sudden, unexpected death of my wife, Janet, whom I had loved for a quarter century, and now, for a second time in three days, these shelves had collapsed. I wondered if there was some connection between these two collapses: if these things, these books, a record of my life, were mirroring the collapse of my soul. These bookshelves were arranged in such a way that they tracked the line of my life; these were the ones that had fallen. And, indeed, after the first collapse my initial effort to restore the order that had been had failed. Were these things of my life speaking to me? Were they perhaps saying the old order is gone, has collapsed, and cannot be restored?

Sitting amidst these broken pieces of my life, I repaired the shelves once again and replaced the books in a random fashion. I made, this time, no effort to arrange them as they had been arranged before. I let the old order die. I let go of what I had wanted. The shelves did not collapse again

Individually and collectively we fear grief and are impatient with it. Everything in our culture is aimed at hurrying us through the process. In the midst of loss I was encouraged by well-meaning and good-intentioned friends to get back into the swing of things. I was told "life goes on." Staying in the land of grief too long, I was, I believe, something of an embarrassment or a threat. I was a walking ghost, an invisible shade, an empty shell with a broken heart. I was a companion of death, and to my friends, a too painful reminder of its presence in the midst of life. Better, then, I was advised, to let the dead bury the dead. Better to forget the loss.

The soul, however, has its own rituals of grieving, rituals which plunged me into the organic rhythms of nature. Loss is a season of the soul—its winter—and, like the winter of the world, a moment whose time must have its place. I could neither hurry nor avoid these rhythms of soul any more than I could hurry or ignore those of the world.

This book is a record of a journey, a journey which I never planned and which was taken without maps. It is a description of the winter landscapes of the soul, that far country where I found myself after an unexpected, sudden, and shattering loss. In this landscape there really are no maps, no markers to plot the course of grief. Here I was forced to find my own way.

But there were stories to accompany me along the path, tales told by those who had returned from the land of grief and who had brought with them an account of their travels. Such stories were not prescriptions for action. They were testimonies which told me that, while I had to find my own way through grief, I was not alone. These stories were markers that said others had already passed this way. They were like a warming fire which brought a measure of comfort in the long, cold nights of sorrow and some small measure of light into the darkness of my grieving soul. In their presence, I could, at least for a moment, rest before continuing the journey into which I had been plunged.

So often in these moments of rest, I felt that my personal grief intersected with a collective one. On these occasions, I was lost in a kind of reverie. Time would slip away, and for a while the boundaries between myself and the world were erased, easing somewhat the cold feeling of isolation which grief brings. In reverie before these warming fires, I could hear those other voices whispering that grief arises because we have dared to love, that grief is the mark of the power of love, to love even when we know that life is loss, to love even though we know that those whom we love will one day pass away.

I am grateful now for these moments, for those simple but eloquent testimonies of love, loss, and grief. I believe they helped me to survive, especially in those early days of grief, and that they gave me some warmth in the longer winter season of mourning. My hope is that the tales of loss and grief which I tell now might do the same for others. They are not intended to be prescriptions for action. They offer no maps. They do not even present a time line of grief and the mourning process, because for me there was no line of progress or development into and out of grief. I can say only that at best these stories record the pattern of my own grief, a back-and-forth movement, like the tides, where the acute shock of grief gave way to the slower, sustained moments of mourning, which at times were followed by a strange sense of peace, a kind of melancholic mood in which loss and sorrow were replaced by something approaching joy, by a feeling of being embraced within a wider field of love, a love which seemed in these moments to be without so much fear of loss. My tales, then, are a testimony to this descent from the early shock of grief into the black holes of mourning and, at times, the unexpected opening into that quiet sadness of melancholy, where I felt a new sense of belonging to others, where a new feeling of hope would emerge, only to be suddenly and even brutally swallowed by a darkness even blacker than before.

While the structure of the book might suggest that grief results in a resurrection into new life, I ask the reader to bear in mind these cautionary remarks: Grief is a wound which leaves a scar, and that scar is forever etched in the fabric of the soul. My stories, then, bear witness to how out of the long, dark winter nights of grief and mourning, I have been able to love again. But they also bear witness to how painfully slow this process is, how the night's darkness never seemed to end, and how I so often lost hope that dawn would ever come.

The initial shattering shock of grief plunged me into the long, slow process of mourning. In the depths of mourning everything I ever was, and everything I ever imagined I could be, was torn away. I fell out of time and the chapter titled Grief and Mourning: The Greening of the Soul is an account of this descent from grief's first awful shock into those mournful depths where for so long I was nothing more than a vegetative existence, where for so long my heart had the hard coldness of the stone. Grief had left me numb, but mourning was a continuous, searing pain. There were times, therefore, when I wished only for that lifeless condition of grief, when I sought oblivion.

Never in the shock of grief, or the longer, slower rhythm of mourning, did I imagine, or could I have imagined, that melancholy could be a fruit of mourning. And yet this is what happened. Not by the force of my own will, but by grace and good fortune, mourning endured ripened into melancholy, where I felt my loss unexpectedly transformed into a kind of peace and wisdom, which, although tinged with sadness, felt like the beginning of a long journey home. The chapter titled "Mourning and Melancholy: The Orphan and the Angel" is an account of this moment of the journey. In these moments of melancholy my grief surprisingly was the path into a connection with the world, a connection which, on the prior side of grief, I had never experienced so intensely. From within the depths of my own grief and its sorrows, I began to sense the appeal of others and even an appeal from the things of the world. It was as if a mood of sadness in blanketing the world was a common bond between me and others, and between me and the world. It was as if my grief and mourning, having plunged me into depths beyond myself, took me out of myself into the world, amplified my being by making me more sensitive and attuned to the pain and suffering of others. In this transformation of mourning into melancholy, I experienced how grief lies in the very marrow of our bones. I was able to appreciate that in the deepest recesses of the heart we are all orphans and that the orphan in each of us carries our shared, collective sense of human sorrow.

AT THE EDGES OF THE WORLD

How long I had sat there was difficult to tell. Only the sense of the late night chill roused me from the twilight state I was in—between sleep and wakefulness. Although this was not the first time I found myself in a place without memory of how or when I had arrived there, on this occasion I felt a fear I had not experienced before. I was sitting in the darkness of the night on the edge of a pier, my legs dangling over the water below.

The water was as black as the late night sky. Frozen between a desire to lean in its direction and fall into its dark oblivion and a fear that I was quickly losing the power to choose to back away from the abyss, I felt something which I had not felt since the moment when my wife died, several months earlier. For the first time since her death, I felt touched by something outside of me. Moved in this moment by the simple presence of the world, I cried. Tears washed down my face, and I realized that I was weeping for something beyond my own sorrow. At the extreme limits of my own grief, I felt touched by a still deeper grief, a grief older than mine, a sadness at the very heart of things, where the ocean itself seemed like the tears of the world, mingling with my own, forging a bond of kinship rooted in sorrow. For so long I had lived with my grief as if I were a ghost, an invisible presence haunting the outer margins of the world. But now in this moment, in the very darkest hour of the night, I felt witnessed by the world, seen in my sorrow, no longer completely alone. And out of this darkness, I heard these words, spoken by the night itself, by the ocean and the blackness surrounding me: "We are all so far from home."

When the sun rose, I inched away from the abyss. And for a while the cold stoniness of grief was warmed by the sun. It was for a moment, and only for a moment, but for the moment that was enough.

Grief had taken me to the edge of the world, and at the abyss I met the Orphan. There at the edge, in a place almost beyond sorrow, I discovered melancholy's wisdom to be a state of the soul where I began to feel beyond the depth of personal loss and, perhaps for the first time, the older, more ancient grief of our shared homelessness. I felt some comfort in how this larger story of grief and loss was able to contain my own grief. Through the Orphan, I understood that my individual moments of loss and sorrow could open onto a wider field. My wife had died, suddenly, and yes, that was a pain beyond anything I had ever experienced or could ever have imagined. She was ripped from life too soon, torn from the fabric of the world at the height of her blossoming beauty. No more would I ever see her welcoming smile. No more would I hear her voice. Alone with this pain, without the deeper story of the Orphan, I would surely have tumbled into the abyss. But in the darkest and most terrible moments of my own sorrow, the Orphan reconnected me to the life of the world.

I say now to my friends that the Orphan who came to meet me in my darkest hour was a figure of grace. Through the Orphan I learned how truly distant I was from myself and others, and how many moments I had let slip by without being closer to those whom I loved. In the presence of the Orphan, I learned too how forgetful I was of my heritage and my destiny and, again, how often I had betrayed myself when I sacrificed my voice for the sake of others. The Orphan kept reminding me that there is true loss and grief in these moments of self-betrayal, when, for example, pulled by convention we turn our backs on a dream, abandon it, let it die. Between commitment and devotion to others and responsibility to oneself, how does one choose? Is something always lost, always sacrificed? Is either family or one's deepest vocation something we leave behind and which must be mourned?

In my own life this education by the Orphan was particularly painful, because my wife died in the midst of this kind of struggle to speak her own voice. At no small costs to herself, she had found her voice, was speaking out, was transforming her heritage into a beautiful destiny. In her mid thirties she had returned to school, finished her undergraduate degree, took a Masters, and was completing her work for a doctorate. In addition, she had helped to write a book on the history of the small city where we were living, doing the archival interviews with its older residents and collecting and researching the photographic evidence of its early years. It was a major achievement for which she was honored at a special ceremony by the city.

This work of finding one's own voice takes courage, a virtue which is rooted in the human heart, as the etymology of the word courage indicates. When my wife died of a heart attack, she was not yet forty-six years old. For so long, and yes, still even now as I write these words, almost seven years after her death, I wonder if she felt too alone in this struggle, if I failed to recognize and support her brave heart. Courage needs love. We cannot do this work of finding and speaking our voice, of being true to our calling, alone. Did I love enough? Was my love too selfish? Was it too much rooted in fear of loss?

The painful truth is that in our last few years together, we were growing closer, and I was learning to be a better lover, friend, and companion. Indeed, on the plaque beneath the tree planted in her memory by my friends and colleagues, I had these words inscribed below her name: "Lover, Friend, Companion, Wife." Their sequence was a tribute to her struggle to grow beyond the conventional role of wife and to find within our relation her calling. Yes, wife she was, but lover first and friend and companion! All of that was gone with her death. Love is so difficult, perhaps the most challenging task of all, because it demands of each of us an openness to the best and worst in the other. Was I too late, then, in learning how to love? I don't know. I just don't know. All I can say is that when the Orphan comes, we learn how impossible it truly is to live a human life in isolation.

How strange to be graced in the isolation of a shattering personal grief by the presence of the Orphan, the one who, being most homeless, is paradoxically the one who most deeply understands the way home. In the presence of the Orphan, I was reminded of how deeply etched the image of home is in each of us, and how wide is its expanse. There were times when in his presence I felt deeply connected to the earth and the animals and even to the angels and the stars. On some of these occasions, the starry night sky was a blanket of comfort, and I felt less cold in my grief, less alone and frightened, less invisible. I remember how I previously used to laugh at Carl Sagan's remark that we are star stuff. But in these moments with the Orphan, I understood what he meant: the way home, which the Orphan in each of us follows, does connect us to the stars. In advance of my grief I could have never known that in grief's stony stillness lay a shining star. Nor could I have known that the Orphan's other face is that of the Angel. How could I? How could I have known that, in the frozen fields of grief's winter mourning, my consciousness would be cracked open and, like a seed, take root in verdant depths which would blossom into angelic heights? In the depths of mourning, I descended into the elements where my consciousness dissolved into its own vegetable rhythms, sank even farther into the hard but brittle endurance of the stone, and then, hammered into fragments, exploded into stars. In that moment of extreme breakdown, the Angel appeared. In that moment of breakdown, the Angel broke through.

THE VOICE IN THE NIGHT

There had been no warning. Only a few moments before, I had greeted my wife at the door, and taking her face in my hands I had said how beautiful she was. She only smiled and laughed that little laugh which so clearly marked who she was, a laugh which blended shyness with a welcoming sense of thanks. Then, suddenly her last words came. "Oh, my God!" she said, and she fell to the floor. I turned in the same instant, and kneeling beside her, I saw her slip behind a veil. I reached out to grab hold of her, to pull her back, an instinctual gesture, but I could not reach the veil which seemed to be there right in front of me but at the same time so very far away. She was fading, becoming less and less distinct, drifting backwards, moving farther and farther away from me, into a kind of dark place. Officially she died some twenty minutes later, but I knew in those first few moments that she was gone, that in passing beyond that veil she had passed into another place.

In the second week after my wife's death, I was awakened by the sound of her voice. She spoke only my name, but her voice seemed to fill the entire room, and what I noticed most of all was the tone with which she called me. Only once before in my life had I heard that tone in her voice, and that was on the occasion when she had gently awakened me from a long sleep shortly after I had been told that my father had died. Her voice on this occasion after her own death had the same qualities of love, tenderness, and compassion and the same soft feel of an embrace, as if the sound itself had a texture to it. And just as I had known that she had died when she passed through the veil, I knew on that night that the tone itself was her message. She had loved and warmed me through my father's death, had awakened me from sleep and called me back into life, and now again she was warming and loving me through her own death, summoning me to awake. She had come back, just for a moment, to ease some of the terrible shock of our parting. Without knowing how I knew it, I knew that this journey, after dying, had not been an easy one for her.

I wanted her to stay, but she was leaving, again. Before she left, however, she gave me another gift. Stumbling from our bed, which so recently we had shared, I walked toward our bathroom to get a glass of water. At the threshold between these two rooms, I felt her hands on my shoulders. Turning around I saw her. She was surrounded by a radiant white light and had increased well beyond the physical dimensions of her former earthly life. I did not think the word "angel," nor did I speak it. But the word was there. She had already taken on the form of her angelic existence.

Larry Dossey, a physician who has written eloquently about the power of prayer in illness, calls angels the missing link. Defending the notion of involution, the downward descent of spirit into matter (a journey opposite the Darwinian notion of evolution with its emphasis on the ascent of matter to consciousness), Dossey says in "Angels: The Missing Link," that "somewhere between the Godhead and that final level of descent, is the angelic domain."[1] I do not know if he is right, and there really is no way of finally knowing, because his claim is not a matter of empirical facts. There is no fossil record left in stone or bone which is evidence of the mark of the angel on us. And yet, somehow we know the truth of this claim. If not in our minds, then we know it in our hearts. This difference between the mind's and the heart's way of knowing seems crucial, and maybe, as Dossey points out, to detect the lingering presence of the angel is a question of how we look, a question of our attitude. Maybe the critical mind is just too inhospitable for angels, too suspicious even of their possibility to give them a place. And, maybe when grief dissolves the mind and its ways of knowing, when we truly do lose our minds in grief, a small space is opened for the angel to appear.

But, again, I do not know. I simply do not know. My wife's voice, however, did awaken me that night, and when I saw her she was different, larger than life and enveloped in a different form. In addition, it was the tone of her voice, and not the content, which called me from sleep. Elaborating his idea that the angel's presence might have to do with how we look, Dossey adds that it might have even more to do with how we listen. The "evidence of angels," he writes, "may be more acoustical than visual." [2]

Perhaps in the final analysis the attuned heart is the necessary condition for the Angel to appear. In grief the heart's song is one of sorrow, a song of lament. Maybe the Angel is especially receptive to us in our moments of pain and sorrow, in our moments of loss and grief. Maybe that is why it seems to me that the Angel is the other face of the Orphan.

Over the course of the years I saw my wife in this guise on several occasions. In addition, as the deep slow process of mourning gave way to melancholy, I saw the face of the Angel many times. I have come to believe that like the Orphan who stands at the abyss, the Angel that waits at the edges of the world, waits to escort us beyond our own personal sorrow, beyond the state of psychological inwardness and isolation. The Angel waits to escort us into a realm which I can only describe as one of cosmological connectedness, into that place where even in that early moment of grief I felt connected with and held by forces beyond the human realm.

I can return now to this sense of being a part of all creation when I look at Van Gogh's painting, *Starry Night*. What must he have felt in those moments under the canopy of all that brilliant light? I find joy and sadness in that painting. Joy, and even a note of celebration, in recognizing that we are star stuff, that something of this heavenly light touches us, that something of the angelic dusts our souls. And sadness in recognizing how far away we are from these moments of connection with all of creation, how our lives here are always punctuated with loss and sorrow, with forgetfulness and isolation. And yet in those moments when I saw the Angel, I knew that our deepest and most painful sorrows can have a spiritual intensity. Through the Angel I learned that personal grief and loss can be moments of potential spiritual transformation.

The third part of this book is testimony to these moments of melancholic peace and wisdom when I felt a new sense of belonging to the world and to others, a springtime of new love. My voice, therefore, is different: here the lament of grief turns into songs of praise

I call these songs of praise lyrical improvisations in celebration of the world. They are lyrical because in the slow transformation of mourning into melancholy, a completely unexpected sense of wonder and delight gradually began to take hold of me. My grief over my wife's death had plunged me into the very depths of hell's darkness, and for a long time I lived only in a state of anger and sorrow. The slowed time of mourning, however, dissolved these feelings, and the tears which for so long had flooded my eyes now seemed to be like the fresh morning dew covering the world. How can I tell you that out of the depths of grief and mourning I began to come to my senses through the rich, sensuous ripeness of the world, that I began to feel in the presence of the simplest things of the world a naive, fresh, and innocent sense of delight, that life again began to touch me like a lover, that from grief there was blossoming a completely unexpected sensual, erotic, and even sexual hunger for the world? How can I tell you all this except in these improvised pieces, these moments of lyrical ejaculation, which celebrate those many moments on those many roads I traveled, which give no reason for them, which offer no explanation of them? I know only that without these lyrical improvisations, this record of my journey through Mexico and Canada, England and France,

Italy and Greece, South Africa and the outer banks of North Carolina, journeys into and through grief, would be incomplete.

And so, I begin in Chapter Five with simple hymns in praise of the small things of the world, with things as fragile as a spider's web, as enchanting as the morning song of the bird, and as awesome as the epiphany of a whale. In their presence, I was often touched so deeply that tears, and not words, were the only initial reply. These tears, however, had a different quality than those which I shed in grief. Even now as I write these words, I feel these tears again, as well as an immense sense of gratitude that our world is blessed by the songs of the birds. The poet William Blake once said that everything in the world is holy. How sad I feel when I realize that I had to lose the one I loved in order to know this simple truth: that the wispy web of a spider, swaying in the wind, is a small miracle. How bittersweet are the lessons of love, loss, and grief.

Chapters Six and Seven of the book recount how these moments of resurrection into life out of grief inspired reveries of endings and beginnings, of origins and destiny. When my wife died, not only did our future die but also our past. I do not mean that my memories of her and of our past disappeared, rather, I mean that without the future that we imagined and dreamed together, the past that we did share changed. It was no longer vital. Without a future those memories no longer made sense, no longer mattered. In my grief I was forced to learn that the past matters only in light of a future and that without such an opening the past is a prison which locks you out of life. If in the early stages of grief, the past and its memories gave me shelter, and kept me anchored in a kind of half-life, there came a point when the past and its memories brought little or no comfort, when in fact those memories only mocked me and filled me with a destructive rage.

CALLING HOME

About six months after my wife's death I began the struggle to gather my wife's things in order to pack and store them. Especially difficult were the moments when I attempted to sort through her clothes, her jewelry, the articles she had written, and the photographs she had taken. Looking at the clothes in her closets, touching them, smelling her presence which still lingered in them, I felt not only my own grief renewed but also theirs. The clothes themselves seemed sad, drained of any life, limp and slack on their hangers. I felt as if they were looking to me for some explanation of her absence. But there was nothing to say. There was only a heavy, gloomy silence between me and her things, and more often than not, I would abandon the struggle, falsely promising to return to it at some later time.

The tape on the answering machine was a possible way to break this silence. In the early days after her death, I would phone the house to hear her voice. But those moments were even worse than witnessing the sad, lifelessness of her clothes. The gap between the recorded message as I was hearing it now, after her death, and as I had heard it before she died, was too great. Then her voice was a promise, even a guarantee, that we would be together. Now her voice only reminded me of the emptiness of the house in which it echoed and the emptiness of my life. Then it was a voice which had a future; now it was a voice with no more tomorrows. The voice on the machine was a dead voice. Without her living presence in the world, that voice was drained of animation. And without her vitality, it became hollow, mechanical, tinny; thin in its sound.

The voice of the dream was more alive; the voice in the dream more real than the voice on the machine. The voice which had awakened me from sleep with the whisper of my name was the true voice now, the voice of my wife in her new form; the voice of a ghost trapped in the machine only mocked that dream voice which had spoken only my name. I stopped, therefore, these phone calls to someone who was no longer there, these conversations without any future, but I never threw the tape away. I couldn't. I could not willingly or actively amputate my past. I could only let it drift away, slip from me in its own time, as I was increasingly swept up in the currents of an on-going life.

To have resisted those currents, to have held onto the machine voice, would have not only kept me a prisoner in my grief, it would also, I believe, have restrained the journey of my wife. Grief and the deep, slow processes of mourning to which it yields have a rhythm of their own, and to refuse to sink into those rhythms is to make a monument of a past which no longer has a future. In addition, I now believe that this refusal injures the dead, holding them in a kind of nowhere, in a limbo space where they are no longer alive but also not truly dead. The dead need to continue their journey, and they need our help to do so. Grieving is not only for us; it is also for them. We help them by surrendering to the natural rhythms of grief and mourning. Out of grief and mourning, we return to life, and we let them go.

Recently I was given an example of this appeal which the dead make to us to grieve and let go. A young woman, whose brother had died in a tragic and unexpected accident, had this dream:

"I am hiking alone behind the Northstar Ski resort when I come

across some ancient ice caves. They are blue and cavernous and deep. I rappel down through chamber after chamber, following the blue light. When I reach the end, there is a room with nothing but a fireplace, which is lit, and a rocking chair. My brother is sitting in the rocking chair. He looks strange because he has a very long, gray beard and his hair looks scraggly. I also notice that his fingernails are grotesquely long. He looks very sad. Once again, I go through the feeling that he is not really dead but has just been here the whole time. I am not angry though. I ask him what he is doing here. He tells me calmly that he is 'stuck here' and that I have to tell Mom to 'let him go.'"

But to yield to grief, to let oneself be taken into its cold, empty places, or to go willingly into that far, winter country of mourning for which there are no maps to chart the way, is almost an impossible task. More often than not I got stuck in my grief, frozen in memories, anchored in the past, and the descent from grief into mourning, where our ties to the past are slowly dissolved, stopped. This work of mourning, a work which is so painful and yet so painfully necessary, an activity which so often felt like a continual tearing at an open wound, often gave way to the leadeness of grief's depression. And even when the work of mourning would begin again, even when, perhaps only for a moment, the ties holding me fast to a dead past were loosened, the shadows of loss would linger. All those yesterdays, which began to change when my wife died because all of our tomorrows were canceled, were not simply erased. On the contrary, they continued to haunt the present and in that haunting, color the future; thus, even five years after her death, when for the first time since her death I forgot to mark the occasion of her birthday, I felt ashamed, guilty for being alive again, and again in love. But should I not also confess here that on that occasion the pain of remembering a past which no longer had a future was replaced by the pleasures of forgetting? Does that sound too uncaring, too harsh, too cruel? I know that I felt that, felt guilty for being in life and love again, felt as if I were betraying my wife and the love we had shared. But I also know that in that moment of forgetting, a cycle of my grieving had come to an end, and that in that ending both she and I were released from a past which no longer had life and were welcomed into a new future.

THE DREAMS THAT MAY COME

The telephone call was completely unexpected. The chairman of the psychology department at Duquesne University in Pittsburgh where I had received my doctorate, had called to inquire if I was interested in returning there to teach. The program had an international reputation, and in the U.S. it was the center for an existential-phenomenological approach to psychology. Almost thirty years earlier, I had begun my graduate studies there, when the department was in its infancy. In that thirty year period, I had established a professional reputation as a teacher and writer in this field, and the call was the fulfillment of a lifelong dream to finish my career in service to this work.

During my first year as a graduate student there, I had met my future wife. Her family had its roots in that city. We married and both of our sons were born there. In so many ways, therefore, I felt that my adult life had really begun in that city, and so much of my sense of self in relation to my wife and family, as well as in relation to my professional identity, seemed firmly rooted in that place. To return there someday would complete the circle of my life.

And now, in the second year after my wife's death

the invitation had come. Not only could I return, but I could do so in a way which honored what I had achieved in the thirty-year journey of my professional life. I still remember, however, the first thought that crossed my mind when my friend called: be careful what you wish for, because it might come true. It was ringing in my ears, like some chorus in a Greek drama, haunting me with its bittersweet tone, with its sense of irony. The invitation was saying, "Return, come home, complete the circle of your life," while the chorus in my head and heart was whispering, "It is too late, the dream is over, you cannot go home again." My wife had died and with her death so too had the dream. The past which we had made there no longer had this return as its fulfillment. That dream emptied into a void.

And yet I could not say "No!" This dream of returning haunted me, like a ghost, and for several weeks I vacillated, unable to make a decision. In the year we had together in California, my wife and I often felt that we were building a new home for the second half of our life. Both of our sons were living elsewhere, and my wife was truly entering into the most creative period of her life, working to complete her doctorate, while being engaged in other writing projects; indeed, just a week before she died, she had for the first time delivered a paper at a professional conference. She told a mutual friend that on the flight back to California she felt as if she was coming home. As I wandered the streets, trying to choose, I felt that were my wife still alive she might choose not to return; indeed, at times I felt her presence strongly resisting this move, as if it would have been a regression for her, a surrendering of her newfound voice.

But I was so lonely now, my life shredded, and the future here so vague and uncertain. Here I would have to make a new life, and I had no maps for what seemed unfamiliar territory. In these moments, everything in me said, "Go back!" Back there lay the security of the familiar, the family, the old city where it had all begun for us when we were still so young. I could return, live a quiet life, and even wait for death to come.

Moreover, my wife was buried in Pittsburgh. That had been a difficult choice. I could not bury her here, where our new life had not had sufficient time to sink its roots deep in the California soil. She would be too alone here, and that thought filled me with too much sorrow. I could not abandon her to a place where no one would remember her. I was haunted by images of a weed-infested grave, unkempt, un-attended, where she would lie for all eternity shrouded in forgetfulness. But I could not bury her back there either. It felt like a betrayal of who she had become and was becoming, as if her burial there would return her to a former life she had outgrown.

In the end, I could not choose, and it was a dream which my wife had about a year before her death that made the choice for me. It was a dream about her grandmother, a person in her life to whom she had always felt very close, and who was for her a kind of soul figure, a mentor of sorts who supported her independence and creative life, the woman who touched her heart. Remembering this dream, and the deep connection between my wife and her grandmother in life, my heart knew they would be close together in death; therefore, I

*had my wife buried next to her grandmother, the place, I
believe, she would have chosen.*

    *In the end I also could not make a choice about the
invitation, and again it was a dream which made it for
me. In the dream, I am kneeling at my wife's grave and
the snows of a November winter are falling on me. The
cemetery is completely empty, the winter sky a steel gray.
As the snow gets thicker, I can feel myself turning to stone,
becoming a granite figure beside her tomb. I awoke from
this dream and I knew that the return would be to a dead
past and that, as uncertain as the future here was, it was
an openness to life. I called my friend and he said he
knew that I would never return.*

    In grief and the long slow process of mourning, the plotlines of
my life were undone, the past that was and the future that no longer
would be were dissolved. I could not have imagined, however, that
from this dissolution of personal time there would arise reveries of
origins and destinies. When my wife died, I fell out of time, and in that
place where time was no more as I had imagined it, where the line of
my life was no longer the sure guide it once seemed to be, I was
returned to the beginning of things, perhaps even to the beginning of
time when origins happen, when founding stories are being made,
and when destinies are being prepared in these beginnings. In the
chapter titled "In the Early Morning of the World," I try to describe
those moments when the world seems new again, when our
experiences seem to open onto the world as if it was just being born in
that moment; thus, a simple experience of light in a valley in Southern
France becomes a reverie not only of the light of my boyhood home
but also of light as the portal or opening to the early morning of the
world. A moment like this has led me to wonder if grief and loss are
the seeds out of which blossom our collective images of Paradise lost,

of Eden and Arcadia, of those places outside time when we dream of our innocence, of those places before time when, as I experienced it, the Angel and the Panther were one, when mind and heart were not yet at war with each other, when the highest in us was still yoked to the lowest, when the instinctual cry of the Animal and the hosanna of the Angel were one voice.

But just as my own grieving has taught me that the past has its value only in relation to a future, I discovered that these reveries of origins make sense only in relation to a destiny which they chart. Images of a beginning are pole stars which guide us home. In a way, therefore, our beginnings are ahead of us, the past comes to us from the future, and Paradise, or Eden, or Arcadia, are not places we have lost or left behind so much as they are beacons which chart the course of our individual and collective lives. In this respect, the death of a loved one is like the disappearance of a heavenly star, and the coming into life out of grief like the birth of a new light in the midnight sky.

In the darkest moments of my grief and mourning, I could not have dreamed that out of grief I would be called back into life through love and that I would experience this love as an enlargement of my being. It is true that we grieve because we have dared to love. But it is also true that we love because we have learned how to grieve. The love that springs anew from grief is more free of fear than love which has not yet been tempered by loss, and in its embrace we recover our citizenship in the cosmos. The chapter titled "Under the Starry Night Sky" tells this part of the story. It describes the other end of the arc of grief and mourning where a psychology of loss is transformed into a cosmology of love, where the wisdom of melancholy, that ripe fruit of the mourning process, allows us to appreciate that we all belong to the same fabric of being, that we are all held in the hands of that supreme mystery of love, and that we are all cradled in eros as the force which pervades all creation. These moments which flower from grief are truly life giving. They are also unexpected, like a gift, and linger only for a short time. But for their appearance and presence I have been and I remain grateful.

INVITATION TO THE READER ~

Earlier I said that the stories that I tell here are testimonies of the soul awakened from grief. They are also appeals. As appeals, these stories are an invitation to the reader to surrender to the soul's rituals of grief and mourning. For this reason, I tell these stories within the mood of reverie, that place where, for a moment, we can dare to let go of what we know and allow ourselves to be embraced by an experience. We know these places of reverie; they take hold of us in ordinary life, in moments, for example, when we are moved even to tears by some powerful piece of music or when we are inspired by a beautiful morning sunrise. In such moments, the boundary which ordinarily separates us from the world is temporarily crossed, perhaps even dissolved, and the burden of identity disappears. In such moments, we feel held and embraced by the world, received and welcomed by the moment, even loved beyond any measure of expectation.

The tales of grief told in this book require this kind of surrender, and thus part two of this book begins with a chapter titled "Dust and Dreams: Reveries at the Heart of Grief." This chapter demonstrates how reverie is a pause, a moment of natural grace which invites us to remember that we are most radically and fully present to others and to the world not by knowing them but by loving them.

But to go willingly and knowingly into that place where we submit to the grieving process is a difficult challenge. It is made even more difficult by the fact that we do not have many, if any, cultural supports for this invitation to yield to grief and its sorrows. The pain and sorrow of grief are so devastating that we prefer to get over them as quickly as possible. In place of surrendering into the experience, we prefer to have the information which would take us past it. In place of being with the grief, we prefer to know what to do about it.

The winter of my soul in grief, however, like the winter of the world, simply was what it was, prior to and always apart from whatever meanings I wished to ascribe to or draw from it, and apart from whatever I wished to do about it. Whatever sense I wanted to make of my wife's death, the force with which grief stormed my soul had its own way. Grief was a tempest which blew apart the fiction of my well-ordered and meaningful life.

The winter of my grief, like the winter of the world, was a slow season. It was a season when sleep and dream beckoned. It was the time when I sought the warmth and comfort of that small fire against the deepening chill of the cold, dark night. The winter landscape of my grief stilled the usual busyness of my life. To be in accord with its rhythm required of me a sense of patience, an ability to wait, a tolerance for the idle hour when I was able to let go of my purposes and intentions. From the outside, this process, which lasted about two years for me, often looked like wasted time. But for the soul it was a time of hibernation when the frayed edges and the worn fabric of my heart were being mended.

Written from this place of reverie, this book is intentionally and deliberately not *about* grief and the mourning process. It is not a how-to book or an information manual which lists the steps which one might take to get over grief. On the contrary, the reveries of grief in this book invite the reader to enter into his or her own grieving experience, to linger with his or her losses, to dwell for a time in the winter regions of the soul. These reveries ask for a curb on that impatience which, as part of our techno-consumer culture, seeks the quick fix for whatever is broken or the easy remedy for whatever is ill. In the tone and style of reverie, this book commits itself to the belief that the grieving soul hungers for the *experience* of mourning and that in the winter of the soul *knowledge* about loss is not enough. In grief's far country, I was not nourished by explanation. In the long winter night I yearned only for the vignettes and the stories that witnessed my experience of loss and echoed its collective depths.

Gaston Bachelard, that great French essayist whose *Poetics of Reverie* have inspired the tone and style of this work, once said that "things, substances, and stars must obey the prestige of their name."[3] In my own grief I discovered that other, larger part of myself which calls me to obey the prestige of my own name as a calling which charts a destiny. The reveries of grief told in this book are a record of my soul's journey home, a homecoming begun in grief and still ongoing, a journey which recounts the black depths of grief and mourning as well as my own sense of becoming one with the cosmos as both a heritage and a destiny. My own name, *Romanyshyn*, means "son of a gypsy," and so I have titled this first chapter "Songs of a Gypsy." These songs, these lyrical improvisations in celebration of that birth of new love and life from grief, are, then, of a gypsy soul which in grief has found its way home. At least for a moment; but for the moment, that's enough.

PART TWO

GRIEF, MOURNING AND MELANCHOLY

Only who with the dead has eaten
of the poppy that is theirs,
will never again lose
the most delicate tone.

~ Rainer Maria Rilke

CHAPTER
2

Dust and Dreams:
Reveries at the Heart of Grief

BEING A GHOST ~

Fragments of phrases, bits and pieces of conversations once heard, once spoken, a line here and a word there, one moment in time and then another, seemingly unrelated, drift into consciousness, coalesce, ignite a spark, and then leave me to wonder about their kinship and affinity. I begin this chapter, pausing to consider two phrases which, in the repose of reverie, whisper their kinship. The first is from William Shakespeare's *The Tempest*. The second is from *Genesis*: "We are such stuff/As dreams are made on."[1] Yes, and if so, then, too, we are dust and unto dust shall we return.[2]

This chapter is an invitation to enter into the mood of reverie, a mood which, I believe, is kin to the mood of grief. In grief you inhabit a nether world between sleep and wakefulness, a place where you are neither in a dream nor fully in the world. You dwell in a moment which is neither night nor day, a twilight world of shadows and light, a world whose darkness is more than the darkest night and whose light is less than the cloudiest of days. In grief, you live in a world where facts do not matter and meanings disappear. Reverie has a similar character. Although I do not know for certain if grief opened me to these states of reverie or if reverie helped me to stay within my grief, I can say that in my heart they belong together.

For so long in my grief I lived in this twilight region, in a kind of state of suspended animation. In this place, the facts surrounding my wife's death held no weight. For months, for example, I carried the autopsy report of her death with me, hectoring my physician friends to read it and explain to me why she had died. They always did so, patiently, but I never felt satisfied by the explanations. On the contrary, the brutal facts only infuriated me, and I felt as if something were missing, something vital about my wife's death which these cold facts could never address or understand.

Nor did the reasons which I attempted to find in order to make some sense of her death help me. For nearly a year after her death, I would write almost daily letters to her, and in them I would engage in a kind of examination of conscience. Had I missed something in our conversations about her struggles with her work? Had I failed to read the signs of her many dreams which we discussed? Was there some purpose to her death, some reason which would make it meaningful? But these too only left me feeling angry and confused. No meaning could erase her death, and no meaning was large enough to hold it.

Both of these efforts, I suppose, kept me more or less sane, but none of it touched my heart. None of this activity matched the mood of my soul, set adrift in the world. I was living on two levels, aimlessly wandering through the day and seemingly organized in those efforts to understand what had happened. Indeed, more than a matter of levels, I was split within myself, fractured at the very core of my being. My body still moved in the world, in a more or less mindful way, but my soul was always elsewhere. I was a ghost, a shade haunting the outer margins of the world. My friends could see me even though I was not really there.

Reverie, like grief, is a way of haunting the world, a kind of consciousness which has slipped from its usual moorings of everyday worries and concerns; it drifts in a mood of detachment among the things of the world. In this condition, I would often find myself experiencing familiar things in an odd way, as if the prescription of my vision had been secretly changed. Of course it had changed. Now my eyes saw the world and its once familiar landscapes through the veil of grief. In addition, small details which heretofore I would never have noticed would suddenly capture me, and, arrested by them, I would wile away an hour or more. Grief had broken the habits of my mind. It had stunned me and shattered the old, familiar contours of my world. In reverie I was experiencing the world as if for the first time, wandering through it with no real purpose or intention. In this mood, dust and dreams betrayed their secrets and revealed their ancient bond. In the depths of grief and in the repose of reverie , I understood that dreams are the dust of soul and dust the dreams of the things of the world. In this small epiphany, of no practical value, I understood more of death than I did with the facts I had at hand or the ideas I had so feverishly constructed. And in this understanding of death, I found a small measure of comfort concerning the death of my wife.

THE ATTIC ~

The attic of a home is the resting place of memory, the place where things, like faithful sentinels, wait for our return. Located at the top of the house, the attic is farthest from the ground of daily concerns and nearest to the sky; it is the place that first receives the warmth of the morning sun and the first to welcome the darkness of the night, the light of the stars, the glow of the moon. What strange alchemy must transpire in that place of silent darkness. What queer and wonderful transformations those things of the attic must undergo, when, farthest from us and released from our presence, they are opened to the stars.

Never before had I wondered what might happen when attic memories are bathed in starlight, when garret dreams are daily warmed by the sun and nightly lighted by the moon. But my grief had drawn me to this place, and in reverie I began to wonder what happens in this place where something of the souls of ourselves is continually exposed to the cosmic night. Gaston Bachelard in *The Poetics of Reverie* writes, "How certainly would the psychoanalysts find new keys for getting to the bottom of the soul if they practiced a little cosmo-analysis."[3]

Perhaps the attic, and not the cellar, is the place where a deep pondering of the human soul should begin. Perhaps the healing of the heart broken in grief begins in reverie and not in our efforts to interpret our tragedies. I don't know. I only know that in grief I lost my mind and that the active pursuit of the facts and the hunt for the reasons why my wife had died, left me only more lost and confused. I know too that it was only in the mood of reverie, in this outwardly appearing aimless wandering, that my soul found its own way of healing. In this mood, the attic became something like a therapeutic chamber for me. Within its space, I found comfort and perhaps, too, a little insight.

A SATURDAY AFTERNOON

I was sitting in the attic, dreaming away, in solitude, a Saturday afternoon. So many things of our life together were gathered in this place, stored, after your death, with careful regard. A quarter century was now housed in this one, singular place, things which were yours, and ours, now wrapped and boxed and placed in this room; waiting for what? For a return of some sort, a return silently promised yet never really spoken at the beginning, when these things were stored here? How long have they waited here in the silence and the darkness, waited for this visit that they might speak again, offer up their secrets, whisper their dreams, release their memories?

There was, however, only silence, and for a moment it felt as if I were among things that had died themselves. But, no!—in truth they had not died; they had only become strange to me. These things, which once held you and me and us together, had only changed. Here in the alchemical chamber of the attic, these things, the former guardians of our memories, had been transformed by the sun, the stars, and the moon. Half in dream, I had entered the garret of my soul expecting to find you again. Instead, however, I found in the attic of the house these things now changed, no longer you, released into something other than what they once were; then, long ago, a living bond between us, and now, in their metamorphosis, witnesses of departure, yours and theirs. These things, like you, had already gone, had already taken on a new life, had already divested themselves of the burden of our memories. In this journey into the attic in search of my memories, I discovered their dreams. In Duino Elegies, Rainer Maria Rilke wrote:

> True, it is strange to inhabit the earth no longer,
> to use no longer customs scarcely acquired,
> not to interpret roses, and other things
> that promise so much, in terms of a human future;
> to be no longer all that one used to be
> in endlessly anxious hands, and to lay aside
> even one's proper name like a broken toy.
> Strange, not to go on wishing one's wishes. Strange
> to see all that was once relation so loosely

fluttering hither and thither in space.
They've finally no more need of us, the early departed,
ones gently weaned from terrestrial things as one mildly
outgrows the breasts of a mother.[4]

> *The early departed finally have no more need of us,
> and in this place of reverie the things in the attic were
> telling me you had gone. More than that, these attic things
> were also whispering to me that without the spark of your
> animating spirit they too were drifting away. All that was
> once a relation between you and them, and between us,
> was now so strangely fluttering in space, ribbons of dust,
> as if the density of things, formerly burdened by the weight
> of our memories, had been lifted from them. In the weak
> light of my attic chamber, I could see fine particles of
> dust moving in the space around me, and I wondered if
> these tiny particles, adrift in the light, were the breath of
> these things. Were these airy, almost weightless particles,
> floating so dreamily in the light, flecks of soul, wispy
> fragments of the soul of these things? Like you, who
> departed too early, did these things no longer have need
> of us?*

In his inspiring book, *The Poetics of Reverie*, Bachelard wonders
what happens when our reveries are spoken. Referring to the one in
reverie as a poetic dreamer, he asks, "Who is speaking, he or the
world?" when the daydreams of reverie become words. "All the beings
of the world," he answers, "if they dream, dream that they are
speaking."[5]

Imagine that when we speak in the repose of reverie our words
are the things of the world speaking their dreams through us. In reverie
we are so close to things that, perhaps, we breathe them into ourselves.
Then, *in-spired* by them, we give voice to their dreams in the next

moment of our breathing, our *ex-piration*. Perhaps reverie is a way of breathing together with the world, a *con-spiracy* between our daydreams and theirs. Human language: the way in which the things of the world whisper through us their dreams; human language as a vessel for the world's dreams!

These are strange notions, but grief turned my world upside down in this fashion. The familiar, ordinary things of life seemed strange, as if they were poised at some odd angle, slightly off kilter, as if the entire world was like a picture on the wall which had suddenly become askew. A disturbance so slight and yet enough to tilt the world off balance, to make everything seem so far away. Indeed, in the first two years after my wife's death there were times in my aimless wandering when I truly did not know if I were looking at things or if things were looking at me, a strange reversal of my usual and familiar ways of being. This same sense of reversal also took place concerning my own voice. At times it no longer sounded like mine, indeed, no longer even sounded as if it came from me. Grief, in fact, had silenced me, had canceled my voice , had taken my breath away. And in this strange place of reversal, things seemed to be breathing through me, speaking their dreams. In the half-light of my attic reveries, it seemed to me that dust was whispering secrets of life and death to me.

DUST

> To whirl about, to shake, to be scattered, dust, in its Indo-European origins, betrays the motion and the movement of things. In the Germanic and Sanskrit offspring of these origins, that motion is a cloud of fine particles blown about like smoke, and in old high German, dust appears as storm and breath. Vaguely aware of these kinships because of my earlier love of language, I began to wonder if dust, that fine layer of

film which so often we sweep away without a second thought, is the stormy breath of things, their very breathing?

I remembered too that dust and fury share the same root and come from the same parentage. Sitting in warm attic light, I imagined dust to be the furious breath of things, and perhaps, too, like the fury of the storm, a breath which was quite wild and chaotic, perhaps even not unlike the cataclysmic energy of those clouds of galactic dust which in their stormy fury birth the stars. The dust which I now saw on those simple things surrounding me—was that too a galaxy of stars perhaps too small to be visible to my seeing eyes, and requiring, therefore, the softer, more open and receptive eyes of reverie? Were these simple things, in their dustiness, a galaxy of stars? Or, perhaps, was it the case that these simple things in their dustiness were betraying their wild dreams of becoming stars? Was the fury of dust the madness of this cosmic dream of things? I thought: are stars and things bonded together as clouds of dust? Is dust that fine film which betrays their kinship? I wondered: when we dust do we disturb a universe?

I sunk deeper into these reveries. As the stormy breath of things, dust reveals its animate character, its vital spirit, its living soul. All of these qualities of dust are evident in its Greek roots where dust collects around itself the trappings of spirit, life, mind, and soul. But dust, I recalled, is also related to dusk, and in this affinity dust belongs to a particular, specific moment in the soul life of things. The layer of dust on these attic things now seemed to me to be the twilight of things, that moment when they seemed to be passing out of their shining wakefulness and moving toward their own nocturnal dreams, that moment when their day seemed to be fading into the night, a moment of change when these dusty things, on the threshold between two worlds, were shedding their skins of meaning and utility, of service and use, and were becoming something other, something of their own, something which now seemed to turn their faces slightly away from me, allowing them to reclaim their own glory.

I felt now as if the attic had become a place of passage, and that the dust, which had settled on these things, was a farewell message which these things that had lingered with me were leaving behind. And yet the trace left behind also seemed to beckon me to follow. I had moments when I thought I glimpsed things glancing elsewhere, and in those moments dust was like a marker pointing me in another direction, taking me beyond myself. Maybe, I thought, dust was even a promise that I was not alone, that I was not abandoned, perhaps even a promise that I did belong to something other and larger than myself. I dreamed that in touching dust, I was touching a tiny particle of soul, and, then, gazing at the Milky Way in the night sky, that spiraling cloudy arm of galactic dust, that I was in some measure connected to the cosmic soul and in some small way was coming home. I knew then that we are such stuff as dreams are made on, and that the stuff of which these dreams are made are flecks of soul, vapors and smoke, that dust which we are and to which we shall return. I knew that when we dust we touch the dreams of things. I knew that when we dust we touch the stars.[6]

THE APPEALS OF REVERIE ~

I left the attic, taking with me this dream of dust and things, and for a while the cold, barren landscape of grief went away. This small opening of the world and its secrets was strangely, even irrationally, comforting. The simple dustiness of things was showing me in a visible way the film of death which covers all life, and it felt to me as if I had had a direct experience of the wheel of life and death which encompasses all creation. True enough, when weighed alongside the brutal absence of my wife, the scales were unbalanced, and this small moment seemed so insignificant. And yet for the brief feeling of peace which it gave me, I felt grateful. Soon enough the world of grief would return, as it always did, as an acute shock of remembrance that my wife was gone, and like some giant stone hammer the shock would again fragment my heart. Against this coming assault which I could feel gathering, like some ferocious wave in the distance, dust seemed a fragile and useless thing, a poor, thin cloth against the cold. Was I not wasting my time in these reveries? Worse, was I not failing to armor myself against grief's shattering return?

The looks on the faces of my friends told me I was, and in their appeals to me to re-enter life, to throw myself back into my work, I could hear their concern that I would be washed away. In these reveries I was open, defenseless, vulnerable. I had lost my grip on things and my foothold in the world. In these moments of reverie, I was standing on a shoreline of shifting sand, the tides of grief continually eroding the once stable, solid ground beneath my feet. And yet, I did not choose to be in this place. On the contrary, it was grief itself which led me to these shores. In a sense, then, I was helpless. I could no more stop this seemingly unceasing rhythm of grief's assaults and its opening of my soul in reverie than I could hold back the ocean's tides, whose relentless pounding at the shore simultaneously gives the shore its shape and form.

For the mind broken in grief, reverie is useless. In a culture which values efficiency and accomplishment, reverie is a most inefficient and unaccomplished way of being, as valueless as dust. Reverie is a prescription only for foolishness and failure. Worse, it is a recipe for disaster and destruction.

And yet grief's heart yearns for reverie and its moments of reprieve. For the soul in grief, reverie is a balm which soothes the pain, the brief moment of respite when all is still, when the world and its demands are briefly silenced. Reverie is a moment when, as Bachelard says in *The Poetics of Reverie*, "facing the great universe of the blank page,"[7] new stars are waiting to be born. In reverie everyday, ordinary things, things as simple as dust, became a blank page, inviting a new start. In reverie I was standing on that shore where the tides of grief were eroding the ground beneath my feet. But for a moment it was the sounds of the tides of grief which mattered. These sounds comforted my tired soul.

FLOWERS TOSSED INTO THE OCEAN

It was the first anniversary of my wife's death. At least that is what the calendar said. In truth, however, the time since her death could have been as short as yesterday or as long as eternity. Grief had left me nowhere, and measured time had fallen away. Only time as endurance remained. In grief, my days bled into each other, and in the states of reverie which it encouraged, moments blended together, where one moment was everything and nothing.

I had gone to the ocean with a bouquet of flowers, with the birds of paradise and the star lilies which were our favorites. I had no real plan. I knew only that I was there at that moment, standing on the shore, holding the flowers in my hand. Although the beach was crowded, I was alone. I hungered for some contact, but I had no voice, no way of reaching across that gap between me and others. How can a ghost be seen or heard by others?

Mindlessly I began to toss the flowers into the ocean. The action took on a life of its own, as if the ocean itself had drawn the flowers from my hands. The waters were saying, "Give these flowers to me, and let my tides carry them to where she has gone." For a moment I felt a quickened pulse of life, a small surge of hope. The flowers and the waters of the sea were bridges connecting our spirits, and I felt that something of my soul could rest in those flowers and be carried with them to the edges of the horizon, to that place just over there, just barely beyond my reach, like that veil when she died—but this time, perhaps, within my grasp, if I could only hold on long enough.

I felt a desperate, wild fury, as if everything now was condensed in this one moment, as if my whole world now was this ocean and the sounds of its waves beating on the shore like a living heart itself. Or perhaps my dying heart was pounding in this way, or perhaps both. The rhythm of the ocean's tides echoed the rhythmic tides of my blood: ocean and heart blending together, life and death mixing their currents in this one eternal moment.

The moment passed. The tides were carrying the flowers back to shore. Behind me the beach was now littered with those water-soaked birds of paradise and star lilies. They looked stupid now, even obscene with their necks broken by the weight of the waves. They looked dead, and I hated them. I hated the ocean too, its thick density too real now, no longer a living heart beating in rhythm to my own broken one. The world, which in reverie had wrapped me in its soft and lovingly tender embrace, was now too loud, too harsh, too brassy, and again too far away. I hated the sun for being so bright.

When the death of my wife plunged me into grief, the world also died. But in the midst of my grieving, small moments of new life occasionally broke through. For me those moments had this mood of reverie, moments when I was escorted into the world's animate presence. In those brief moments, I saw the things of the world as if for the first time, as if I were seeing them in their original epiphanies, as if grief had scoured the scales of forgetfulness from my eyes. I could witness things blossoming with their own vitality, long before I had learned to make them useful by ascribing to them my intentions and meanings, by imposing upon them my will. Grief had broken my will, and in reverie the soul was saying to me, "Not your will, but let my will be done!"

Like grief, these moments of reverie undid me. The once familiar landscapes of the world, the things I counted on, assumed, and took for granted, were dissolved in grief and in reverie. But where grief attests to the dying side of life, reverie attests to the possibility of some new life. I would not say, however, that with reverie came hope for new life. Rather, I would say that with reverie there came a startling sense of wonder in the face of life at all. In reverie I felt called to be so close to things that I was impregnated by their spirit and reanimated by the force of their life. In this respect, reverie was for me the other side of grief's dying: grief's constant companion in the soul, its twin.

In grief the meanings of my world disappeared; while in reverie the world blossomed as a welcoming mood. Flowers tossed into the ocean promised to carry my soul to that other place where my wife was waiting for me, and the ocean spoke, inviting me to surrender to its will. In reverie I was taken behind or beyond what things mean to how they feel, to how they touched and moved me.

Reverie is a mood of the soul which is prior to the logic of the reasonable mind. When I lost my mind in grief, I fell into these moody depths of the soul and in these depths I was present to the world not as a matter of meaning but as a matter of beauty. I do not mean that the world suddenly became pretty. Beauty is not really about that at all. Rather, I mean that the world suddenly became an awesome presence, and on these occasions the sheer abundance of life in all its variations overwhelmed me. Grief had already stripped me of my defenses, made me raw and vulnerable, and in reverie the naked vitality of the world assaulted me. In these moments, I no longer had the armor of my ideas about things and the world. I was no longer able to make sense of things, I could only sense them. Rainer Maria Rilke knew this awesome power of beauty, when, in reference to the angel's beauty, he wrote in *Duino Elegies*, "Beauty's nothing/but beginning of Terror we're still just able to bear."[8]

Reverie is a surrender of the desire to *know* things so that we might once again, at least for a moment, *be* with them. A knowing which springs solely out of utility always needs and wants to do something with what it knows. Reverie is a way of being present to the world which wants nothing and needs nothing from things. In this respect, it is so much like the world of grief, when I wanted nothing because I was nothing.

Rilke, again, captures this difference between knowing things and being with them. His *Duino Elegies* are a testament to a lifetime of struggle to stay close enough to things so that he could echo their song. These ten elegies are to poetry what Beethoven's symphonies are to music: a witnessing presence to the sublime heights available to the human spirit when it stays so near the world that it can open itself to be touched by the dreams of things.

For Rilke, a knowing which strives too early and too insistently toward meaning sets us up *before* the world, positions us in front of it, leaving us a little less in the world. Reverie reverses a little, at least for a moment, this betrayal of the presence of things into premature meaning. Loosening its ties to a language which makes sense of the world as a map or mirror of our minds, reverie speaks because first it has listened. It speaks out of a contemplative silence which echoes the breathing soul of things. Reverie is the voice of dust and clouds, flowers and the ocean, stars and stones, the colors of nature and the terrible presence of the Angel speaking through us, lending us in return something of their animating spirit. When words flow from reverie, when, haltingly, we begin to find a voice again in grief, we can wonder who now is speaking. Henri Bosco in *L'antiquaire* says, "All the being of the world, if it dreams, dreams that it is speaking."[9] Grief, and the mood of reverie which is its companion, lets us in on this secret kinship between us and the world. The French poet Alain Bosquet captures this bond when he says,

> "It is an honor to be the wind
> It is a happiness to be the stone."[10]

My reveries in grief were a moment when I was in-spired again by the world, a moment when the world breathed its soul and new life into me. In this sense, these moments of reverie in grief seemed to me to repeat the original act of creation, when the breath of God stirred the dark waters of the void. This is why, I believe, Bachelard says that reverie has no purpose other than "to put us into the state of a soul being born," and that it has no meaning other than to enlarge our lives "by letting us in on the secrets of the universe." To know, for example, that dust is the dream of things will not make me richer or more accomplished or a success. To know, for example, that when I dust I disturb a universe of stars, is useless. But it is exactly this uselessness of reverie which is its value, this uselessness which rescued, for a moment, my heart broken in grief from its more familiar obsessions with purpose and utility. In grief, my life became a heavy blanket of sorrow. Reverie functioned "to liberate [me] from the burdens of life."[11]

Poets have always understood the valuable uselessness of reverie, and in the depths of my grief it was the poets who saved me. Every day I would read out loud some words of this or that poet, and it was the absence of advice which comforted me. I did not have to struggle to take anything in, to make some sense of it, to make it fit the loss I had suffered. No, it was enough just to hear the sound of the words, and to be held in the rhythm of language, this first level of vitality where I was seduced by the flow of language, by its animating force before I had to ask what words might mean. And it was the sound of my own voice surprising me, coming from some different, unknown place, strangely familiar and eerily strange: only sound and rhythm, primitive, even barbaric, shouting sometimes the words, or making wild whooping noises with the words, as if this language spoken in reveries in grief was not yet fully human, as if it still retained some animal cry in it. These moments of reverie in grief instilled a deep hunger for raw life, and when these moments would overtake me, it was only poetry which fed my hunger. Not surprisingly, then, I grew thin in body but thicker in soul.

The poet E.E. Cummings addresses this difference between a hunger for life rooted in the vegetable and animal rhythms of the soul and one rooted in the mind and its later appetites for knowledge. In a group of poems titled *is 5* he writes:

> since feeling is first
> who pays any attention
> to the syntax of things
> will never wholly kiss you.[12]

The syntax of things! This kind of knowledge comprehends how the world is put together; it contains a certain utilitarian value not to be scorned. But such a knowledge already places us in a different kind of relationship to things than reverie does, and by itself it is not enough. In grief I needed something more than to know how the world works and how it is put together, especially when the world I had known had exploded apart. I needed to be embraced by what I loved, to feel held, and even to be kissed by the world. And that is what these moments of reverie did for me. In the same group of poems Cummings writes:

> (While you and i have lips and voices which
> are for kissing and to sing with
> who cares if some one-eyed son of a bitch
> invents an instrument to measure Spring with?
> each dream nascitur, is not made...)
> why then to Hell with that: the other; this,
> since the thing perhaps is
> to eat flowers and not to be afraid.[13]

Imagine knowing spring by eating flowers! Like knowing the stars perhaps by making love! Each dream "nascitur," he says. Each word is born through us, not made by us. Knowing the world, like knowing spring, is the fruit of a coupling. In grief I was forced to come to terms with the brutal fact that I am not really in control of my life, and that no matter what I might do I cannot save anyone from their fate, least of all those whom I love. Grief blew apart my familiar world and forced me to recognize that I am not as much the author of meaning as I had believed myself to be. Rather, I am more like an agent of meaning, the means by which the dusty dreams of the things of the world are realized.

Reveries in grief took me into this strange place of reversal where the terrible, lonely isolation of grief did open up to a sense that I was held and loved by forces larger than myself and which I could not ever fully understand. In this regard, the primitive vitality of poetry cut below what my mind knew, and would seek to know, about grief and easing its pain. Poetry's raw vitality spoke to my heart shattered in grief, to my soul shipwrecked in sorrow. To my mind cracked by grief, poetry offered no proof that life would come again. But it did offer some promise that it might. To my mind tormented in mourning, poetry offered no facts to ease the pain. Rather, it offered a kind of dumb, animal faith that life does endure. In the depths of my grieving, promise and faith were as fragile as dust and nothing when measured against the density of proof or the hard certainty of fact. But that is all that I had—dust and dreams!

Reverie is the other face of our technological culture which eschews grief, because it has no time for its pain, and which avoids mourning because it is impatient with its slow pace. It is the other face of a techno-culture which separates us from the world so that we are not touched and moved by its strange appeals. Reverie slows us down, as grief assuredly does, and helps us to remember that in the marrow of the bone we have a deep hunger for the world, an appetite which in some dim praise and even envy of the animal, makes us long at times to be sky and tree, bird and star, ocean and wind. I know that I felt this hunger many times, and at other times felt the fulfillment of that longing, felt the wonder of being a stone, rooted, enduring, but silent, deaf to everything, even if only for a moment, folded contentedly within a deeply felt sense of place. I know that there were times in the two winters of mourning that I did feel the intense, enduring peace of the stone.

Reverie put me in touch with these moments, with these yearnings to let go of my mind and all that I had placed between myself and life. And grief, a kind of uninvited but enforced reverie, threw me into these same moments when its terrible storms ripped apart my mind and I fell, uncontrollably, into a kind of vegetative state, where all movement stopped and I simply endured the storms.

WINTER

> *A beech tree in the garden of a house in a small village on the northern coast of Devon, England. A cold November morning. The tree is bare, but its empty brown branches design a stark mosaic against the bleak winter sky. The morning light is weak, pale, and drained of any color; the gray sky, burdened with heavy clouds, only intensifies the sharp outlines of the twigs and branches, the arms of the tree with delicate fingers at rest in winter repose. The simple elegance of this lone tree against the washed out sky arrests my eye: a plain mosaic of black and white, a visible haiku, a poetry of form, the animate geometry of nature. In looking at this tree I long to be a painter. Cezanne once said that all he ever wanted to do was to capture one moment of the world's being. This mosaic is just such a moment.*
>
> *But I am no painter, and besides even the great Cezanne painted Mount Saint Victoire some eighty-six times, trying to capture that one moment. What was it that the poet Rilke said of Orpheus? Raise no monument to him? Yes, but let it be the rose, he said, which in its blooming is already fading.[14] Eruptions of the world's being, always in moments of unguardedness, always when one is not looking for anything but is open and already near dreaming, need first and perhaps only our witnessing. Later, when we have been sufficiently penetrated, a word or a color on canvas or a note on a flute might be made.*

So I sink back into myself in front of this tree, gather myself against the morning chill, hunch my shoulders, and feel myself becoming increasingly still and silent. In the presence of this great being, the tempo of my own life is slowing down, resonating in harmony with the reduced rhythms of the tree, blood and sap flowing at the same languid pace, the difference between them fading, a boundary being crossed, now erased, as if the two juices are mingling together, as if one flow is now circulating between us. It is a moment of possession, and I know that I could become inert, like a stone, or fall into the winter sleep of this tree. I could release to these ancient rhythms, and I want to, to let go of wakeful consciousness and become only an element, a part of all this wintry slumber, content only to wait, to sleep, to dream. This vegetable siren is waiting for me. It welcomes a surrender with that infinite patience which has marked its rooted endurance to this place where (for how long now?) it has welcomed winter snows and dreamed its winter dreams. One moment, exactly this moment, now becomes an eternity, and between each beat of the heart, eons can pass. I have been here before. I have been here forever, blanketed in winter snows, cousin to this tree, kin to this patient sentinel waiting my return.

About two and a half years after my wife's death, I had traveled to England. The woman who two years later I would marry was living there. But at this time we barely knew each other. This visit was a wild, uncharted journey. I was drawn to this landscape of wind and storm, of cold nights and early darkness, and to a woman who lived there and roamed the hills. In this setting I could become part of the sap that strengthens the rose, and could feel the blood pulsing through my body reverberating with the thick, heavy juices that throb through stem and leaf and turn the flower toward the sun. In *Les Memoires d'Adam*, Pierre Albert-Birot says "the world enters me like the fruits that I eat; [in reverie] I nourish myself with the world."[15] On this cold November morning, this barren tree of winter was feeding my soul. A mosaic of my soul, it spoke to my own grief as a time of enclosure, and held for me those images of mourning's long, cold, dark, winter nights, a season of patient endurance. It spoke to me too of how it had borne its own frozen life with dignity and simple, elegant grace. In its presence my own grief and mourning were given back to me in its natural rhythms, as a time of conserving, of storing up deep within the heart a small glow of life, a blue fire whose low heat radiates an interior warmth against the worldly cold. This barren tree was the winter of my soul, a season of solitude, a time for recollecting what had been lost and left behind.

If grief has a landscape, and I am certain it does, then it might very well be a simple winter hut in a snowbound forest, a hut whose light and heat are enhanced by the cold outside, intensified into an interior coziness which invites the grieving soul into reverie. In this quiet landscape, grief's far country, I rested between loss and gain, and I realized, perhaps for the first time, that life is loss and that everything that is present to us is always shadowed by absence. Even the simplest things, like a chair or a table, or a lamp or a desk, seemed haunted by some invisible bond which turned their faces away from me, giving them a faraway look. It is as if they have heard the call of some distant kin, like dust rising toward the stars. In these quiet moments of my grief and its reveries, I knew how fragile the worlds are that we build for ourselves, that in gaining a world we too often lose the cosmos. We lose a sense of connection with the rest of creation and forget that the red blood which courses in our veins is also the green sap which flows in the veins of the tree. Rilke describes this connection in the tenth of his *Duino Elegies*:

> We wasters of sorrows!
> How we stare away into sad endurance beyond them
> trying to foresee their end! Whereas they are nothing else
> than our winter foliage, our somber evergreen, *one*
> of the seasons of our interior year, — not only
> season—they're also place, settlement, camp, soil, dwelling.[16]

This book is written in reverie where we are not "wasters of sorrows." It offers no maps for the mind to find its way in the winter country of grief. But it does invite the reader to fall into the soul of grief and surrender to the soul's way of traveling the cold, dark roads of grief and mourning. Stories along the way, forged and told from this place of reverie in grief, ease the journey. These stories, told around a small fire in the winter country, allow for a moment a pause before the journey of grief continues. They create a place to stop, rest, linger and recollect for a moment what has been left behind in one's loss.

CHAPTER

3

Grief and Mourning:
The Greening of the Soul

Why do leaves commit suicide
When they feel yellow?

~ *Pablo Neruda*

SWEET OBLIVION ~

Long ago, in a world that shades into the time of myth, there was a great poet. His name was Orpheus, and his words were so sweet that they had the charm to make the willows weep. Orpheus was also a lover, and his wife Eurydice was his greatest love. But one day she died unexpectedly and Orpheus was inconsolable. With his sweet words, however, he descended to the underworld, and there he persuaded the gods and goddesses to release his beloved from the chains of death. They granted his request, but they laid upon him one condition. On his journey from the underworld, Orpheus was forbidden to look back to see if Eurydice was following him. At the last moment he faltered. He turned and in that moment Eurydice faded away, back into the land of the dead, forever.

The story suggests, I believe, that in the face of the utter finality of death words fail. Not even the greatest of poets and lovers was able to rescue his beloved from the arms of death. Death demolishes any hopes we might have about overcoming loss or controlling its pain. In the face of death's total victory there is only endurance and, if one is lucky, grace. Death dissolves into the elements the flesh of the one who has died. It does the same to the mind of the one who goes on living. In this place of dissolution we are beyond making sense of who we are, who we have been, who we might be. In this place there is only silence. Later, perhaps, a word or two might come, but only after the experience of the dissolution of one's self into the dumb, dark rhythms of the natural world.

The reveries in this chapter are the few words I have found to describe the descent into the elements, that moment when the initial shock of grief gave way to the long, slow winter of mourning. They fail, as they must. But without them something of the journey of my soul through grief and mourning would be lost.

GREEN

> *It was a late Sunday afternoon, warm, the sun poised in the middle of the sky as if it had not yet made up its mind to surrender to the night. The color of the light had a texture to it. I felt strangely at peace in its warm embrace. How long I had been sitting on a bench within this field of soft light, I could not say. It might have been minutes or hours. It could have been days or even an eternity. I was myself, there on that bench, and I was also this light, spread out across the green fields of grass and trees. More than a year since my wife had died, this moment was a welcome surprise. From a place deep within my soul, I felt something budding within me, as if a shoot of the vegetable world was breaking through the hard crust around my heart, struggling alongside the brute, dumb power of nature's life to leave the darkness of the earth and be warmed by the sun.*

The green field of grass spread out in front of me began to undulate. Waves of pure greenness were pouring out of the bushes and trees, vibrating in some kind of wild ecstatic dance of freedom. It was as if greenness itself had escaped its forms in blade and leaf, in stalk and stem. No longer bound by form, color was shamelessly revealing itself in riotous, even erotic, abandonment. Green! A deep, rich, fresh, moist, wet, dripping, green! A blue-green, yellow-green, green-green! A green so green that only the sky could be more blue. Pure color, yes!, but with it the pungent smell of the vegetable body. A heavy, cool, damp odor penetrating the cold corners of the dark interior jungle of life, green was displaying itself as the swelling force of the vegetable body. Green: a tumescent, throbbing pulsation; a rhythm, a tempo, a pace, a speed, a quivering, a small shudder of the body of creation. A frequency, a vibration, a radiance of the world's consciousness, perhaps even the first vibration of life. Something in me wondered if color is itself a kind of consciousness, and if consciousness, my own consciousness in this moment, is only another, different frequency of color. Green, yellow, blue, red, purple, orange: variations in the harmonies of a consciousness spread throughout all creation, enfolding mind in nature.

Freed of form, color was dancing with the light. The field of green before me was dissolving into an expanse of shimmering diamonds, crystals of radiant light catching the sun then releasing it. The field of green was alive, and I knew, without knowing how I knew it, that color was life.

I wanted this moment to last forever. The continuing despair I felt over the death of my wife was unbearable, and I wanted to be rid of it. An urgency took hold of me. Here in this moment I felt alive and visible, and I needed someone to see me, to witness that I was still in life, not dead, no longer a ghost. The ice around my heart was melting away, warmed by the sun and the fierce, deep fire of green. Green was penetrating me with its life, with its throbbing vitality. Held in its grip, I felt my soul, perhaps for the first time since my wife had died, turn toward life, like the vegetable world turns toward the sun. This green life pulsing through me was a tropism, a primitive hunger asserting itself, an elemental force even deeper than the instinctual, a vegetable vitality even older than the vitality of the animal.

Propelled from the bench, my arms were spread open by the wide sky, and from this wild, ferocious place, without reason or caution, words of love were disgorged from my mouth. From the depths of green a cry of love burst forth, and that small part of me that was still my conscious mind hoped that its vegetable force would carry it across the ocean to the woman I had recently met and who was now living in England.

Ensconced in folklore, the Green Man is an icon who reaches out to us from the depths of prehistory. Either as "a male head formed out of leaf mask," or "a male head disgorging vegetation from his mouth and often from his ears and eyes,"[1] the Green Man is the explosive exfoliation of all life, the omnipresence of renewal and rebirth. To scholars of myth he "symbolizes the union of humanity and the vegetable world,"[2] and while that is true, it is also incomplete. The greenness of the Green Man is something wholly other before it is

ever an icon or a symbol for our minds. The greenness of the Green
Man is a pre human, or a proto human force. It is elemental: the iron
in our icons, the sap in our symbols

The greenness of the Green Man is a vibration of consciousness
itself, a punctuation in the multiple frequencies of consciousness which
comprise all creation, a moment in consciousness which is older than
the frequency of our conscious minds. Green is a wisdom of its own,
older than ours, a green wisdom which is always there, always present
and throbbing at the core of our being. It is what Hildegaard of Bingen,
that remarkable woman from the thirteenth century whose songs of
life and love and loss have emerged in our own time, called *viriditas*
(greenness), her name for the cosmic energies of all creation.[3]

Green is an intelligence built into creation itself, and I was partaking
of it in this moment of shipwreck or breakdown, when my mind could
do nothing else but surrender to its vegetable allure, when it could do
nothing else but lie in its vegetable charms. It was this dark wisdom of
which we are not the makers which cracked open the hard shell of my
grief. It was this elemental force, this throbbing river of life, which
dissolved the icy numbness of my grief and simultaneously plunged
me into the deeper and more lasting state of mourning. As much as I
wanted this moment of green and its eruption of life to last, it proved
to be only a moment. The green force of life had taken hold of me,
had shaken me to life in my grief, but only to pull me deeper into
those dark, underworld depths of mourning.

This chapter is a description of the longing for oblivion which haunts
the slide of grief into the protracted state of mourning. By oblivion I
mean that yearning for the siren song of sleep, a hunger so deep that
it even passes beyond any active pursuit of it. In my grief there were
many moments when I could no longer summon the energy even to
soak my consciousness in wine. I was beyond any kind of caring about
what I did. I simply vegetated, sat still like a stone, and hoped that the

next breath would by my last. It was not that I wanted to die. It was just that I was too tired to live. In these moments I was ripe for a takeover by the elements, by those forces of nature which were certainly older than my mind, stronger than my will, and wiser than my heart. Even something as simple as green offered this sweet oblivion. It possessed me, and I could simply let go and fall into its primitive rhythms. The fall, however, was farther than I ever could have imagined.

In these reveries of mourning, I do not offer a psychology of grief. Rather, I offer something closer to a poetics of the elemental forces of life which lie beyond psychology. In its worst moments, psychology can be an obstacle to these elemental epiphanies because it appeals too much to the mind and its desires to understand and control. But in its best moments, psychology can be a preparation for the disclosures of these natural forces of the soul, disclosures which can often have a numinous quality to them, a sense of something divine or holy.

As strange as it may seem, grief can be such a moment of disclosure. Loss can lead to a transformation which is so profound that the bereaved one appears to those who have known him as another being. Indeed, on one occasion a very close friend of mine told me that I was beginning to frighten people, because, as she said, I had the look of someone who had had a glimpse of some other world. She said I looked like some wild, holy man who had descended from the mountain with a vision too terrible to tell. Well, in fact, I had, and I had no words for it. But often I could feel it in my eyes, as if they were possessed by some ferocious fury that would inflame what they saw. In these moments, I was truly beyond myself, taken over by these elemental forces working their way into and through me.

THE COCOON

I was cast up upon this shore by fate. My wife's death felt like a shipwreck of my soul. I was marooned, isolated from the mainland of daily life. Cut loose from my moorings by her death, I was without any anchor in the world, prey even to the smallest breeze or shift in the tides. I was drifting. I had nothing to do, and, almost out of spite, cared to do nothing. There were no plans to be made, no actions to take, no summons which reached me from the side of the world. In shipwreck, I had become deaf, and the world had grown silent, as if it were now blanketed by a heavy snow. But in the deepening silence I could hear the strange and terrible voices of the elemental world, and I knew that these forces were coming to get me. So often, my only response was to crouch in some corner of a room. I was afraid.

Mourning is shipwreck. Unlike grief, mourning has a different feel to it. Where grief is more sudden, like a thunderbolt, mourning seems more like a long, hard, dark rain. Where grief is quite often accompanied by a kind of numbness, mourning seems closer to that condition of oblivion, where one is beyond even the absence of feeling. Grief leaves traces of the human realm in you, but the deep, slow process of mourning is elemental. In mourning, I was truly losing my grip on the world. I was even beyond suicide, for that act would have required of me some energy which I no longer had. I was slipping away into a kind of madness which reached deep into my blood and bones, a cellular madness which plunged me into the core of the soul and fused me with that awful, vegetable force of the green world. This green world was encroaching upon me with that same pounding, merciless energy which the composer Igor Stravinsky had captured in *The Rite of Spring*. It was gathering its fury with that same ruthless insistence which the poet Dylan Thomas describes in "The Force That Through the Green Fuse Drives the Flower."

The force that through the green fuse drives the flower
Drives my green age; that blasts the roots of trees
Is my destroyer.
And I am dumb to tell the crooked rose
My youth is bent by the same wintry fever.[4]

The mourning process is a greening process, and green consciousness, that force which drives the flower and runs deeply and silently in our own veins, plunges into the dark soil of the earth, where all is night. In these vegetable veins "circulate the juices drawn up from the rocks and realms of the mole, the worm and the microorganisms of the soil..."[5] Now I was there, in that night below the earth, where I felt the greening of my soul begin. In these dank, dark green depths of the soul in mourning, I heard only the sound of myself being enwrapped within a vegetable cocoon. The sound, like green leaves being torn from a ripened ear of corn, filled my ears, flooded the house, and echoed in the world. I could not escape it, even in sleep. It was a mournful dirge, a death song being sung for me, the threnody or funeral hymn of my transformation into vegetable life, the sound of my own soul becoming green. Do you believe me when I tell you that I could tell no one of this because I was struck dumb by it, like Dylan Thomas says with respect to the crooked rose? That elemental force which blasts the roots of trees and is our destroyer is not something with which we have a conversation. I was beyond language as this green vegetable force in the dark night of the earth worked itself into my flesh, pierced my skin, cracked my bones, and soaked up the blood in my veins.

In the elemental world of the mourning soul, time moves very slowly. Measured by the clock, I was gone perhaps for a day or two at different moments. But measured by the rhythms of the soul, I lay in my vegetable cocoon for an eternity. Eons had passed, and in this space my thoughts evaporated, my mind stopped, and only sensuous awareness remained. There were sounds, smells, tastes, textures, but it was not me or my personal mind which experienced them. Instead, there was a kind of identification with them, so that in these moments the boundary between myself and the world disappeared. 'I' was the breeze that only slightly disturbed the leaves of 'my' vegetable tomb. 'I' was the warmth that only barely penetrated the depths of 'my' vegetable coffin. 'I' was the rain that gently washed the skin of 'my' vegetable body. Light, darkness, warmth, cold, rain, snow— in these moments only these cycles of hours and seasons mattered. But they mattered in their fullness, so that within these cycles each ray of morning light was exuberance, a moment when tomb seemed like womb. That first moment of warmth, of low heat after the cold darkness of the night, and every first moment of morning, was always a primal beginning. Each morning moment was all of creation, all of time living in that one moment—every time, every morning, each morning the whole, every morning this first beginning. My green soul—raw, new — was singular and complete in this way, without the horizons of memory or desire. Tucked within the rhythms of the world's green being, woven into the vegetable fabric of creation, the 'I' who was the weaver disappeared.

Mourning, I now believe, bathes the soul in the ancient, slow rhythms and the deep wisdom of the green world. The German poet Heinrich Heine spoke of this wisdom in imagining the dream of a tree. Imagining "an isolated spruce slumbering under the ice and snow, lost in solitude upon an arid northern plane," Heine wondered if this "spruce dreams of a palm tree which, way off in the distant Orient, grieves, solitary and taciturn upon the slope of a burning rock."[6]

Commenting on this image in *The Poetics of Reverie,* Gaston Bachelard reminds us that in Heine's native German the spruce is masculine and the palm feminine. Then Bachelard wonders: "What a lot of dreams are directed toward the feminine tree, open in every one of its palms, attentive to every breeze." That feminine tree, that palm of the Orient, that exuberance of green toward which the winter spruce directs its dreaming, Bachelard rightly calls a "vegetable siren."[7]

In mourning, my soul was called by this vegetable siren, by the green of the world, lured by its wet, pungent odors. Penetrated below my mind by its damp, moist morning mists, my mourning soul was wrapped within its odorous embrace. For a long time, for a time beyond measure, I stayed there, as if my soul had found after shipwreck this safe harbor. But the soul in mourning has its own wisdom, and again the 'I', that small piece of me which still remained, was further undone. The mourning process did not end for me in the vegetable world, in the world of green. No! Green rots. It decays and it too surrenders to something older than itself.

THE WORM, THE STONE, AND THE ANGEL

I lay there, lost in the slow rhythms of green. Snow had come, blanketing my vegetable coffin. The rains of spring had come and washed it clean. Night had come, so many times, with its frigid darkness. The morning sun had come and had warmed vegetable dreams. How long I had lain there, resting deep in vegetable sleep, watched over by a mineral wizard, a stone guardian, did not matter.

The descent was a precipitous fall. My vegetable body began to rot. Green had turned to spots of brown and yellow. Plummeting deeper and deeper into the soil, my cocoon coffin began to mingle with the dark matter of the earth. Termite and ant, mole and worm, feasted on the remnants of my vegetable body. The cocoon above had collapsed. The Mineral Wizard stood alone.

Falling deeper, deeper into the blackness of earth,

> *my vegetable self decayed. 'I' was becoming stone and*
> *rock, pebble and mineral, and green now seemed so far*
> *away. Had green always been only a mineral dream?*
> *Mineral being, only shape and texture and the awareness*
> *of a brittle, hard endurance.*

The slow, deep rhythms of mourning had now taken me beyond the green world into a place of stony silence and stillness. 'I' longed only for sleep and indeed for a state beyond sleep, for that eternal oblivion of the stone. From this place even the green world seemed to be filled with too much life and mind. In one of his poems from *The Book of Poverty and Death*, Rilke speaks to this image of the stone:

> It's possible I am pushing through solid rock
> in flint like layers, as the ore lies, alone;
> I am such a long way in I see no way through,
> and no space: Everything is close to my face,
> and everything close to my face is stone.[8]

Mourning is a descent into the unconscious, that murky domain of experience which has been the province of psychology. But even my long years in service to psychology was of no help to me in this descent. What did psychology know of the green world of the soul in shipwreck, and what could it say to me of these even older, deeper layers where the soul in mourning takes on its crystalline form? Could I say to my colleagues, or to anyone for that matter, that I was a stone, that I could feel the slow heartbeat of stones, and that I yearned to fall into this place of sweet oblivion? How could I tell them there were days when the only thing I could do was to press myself against a stone, embrace it, and wish to become one with it? At this level explanations, ideas, theories could not reach me, let alone save me in any way, because everything that was happening to me seemed beyond meaning. Even the kindest and most sincere attempts at understanding seemed more than useless. They seemed offensive.

My heart, torn asunder by grief, was submerged in the ever slower rhythms of mourning. This breakdown of mind opened the door to these other, archaic forms of consciousness. In this largely uncharted domain, the only thing I could do was endure. The shock of grief and the descent into mourning had taken me to the far edges of the human world. Beyond its boundaries lay a world of forces beyond my powers of control. In these regions I was in the care of the Green Man and the Mineral Wizard, and my heart, my formerly human heart, was now beating in harmony with the vegetative rhythms of the green world and the even slower rhythms of the world of stones. Green tendrils broke through my scalp and burst from my nose, and their damp, pungent odors soaked my pores. The orbit around my eyes hardened into granite, sealing me in a stone prison increasingly distant form the human world. Submerged in the green juices of the vegetable world, and encased within the hard interior of the stone, I was shrinking away. The 'I' whom I formerly was was dissolving into 'i'.

> *It came without warning, only a sound, a terrible wind, followed by a shattering explosion. Flecks of mineral, tiny crystals, tumbling and twisting, were being swept along in a sea of streaming energies. Pulses of light flashed from this sea and, at what seemed like the outer reaches of infinity, tumbled into a void. In the void all was silent. Only a vast and empty darkness was there. This was eternal night feeding itself on the light, a dark hunger, as limitless as all creation, devouring the energies that were pouring into it. This night had always been, and it would last forever, a deep, dark nothing at the heart of creation.*
>
> *But the sound returned, and the belly of night erupted. A whole universe of light was blinking into being; a whole*

> *universe of light and life was being born from the*
> *hammered fragments of the mineral body and out of the*
> *darkness of the night.*
>
> *Green had rotted and decayed. The vegetable world*
> *had fallen into mineral dreams. Now stone had exploded*
> *into ribbons of energy and, swallowed by eternal night,*
> *had become a universe of stars. These stars, too, like*
> *everlasting night, had always been. This universe of stars*
> *in this black sea of empty space had existed since the*
> *beginning of time, which had just begun.*
>
> *From the center of this field of stars a brighter*
> *radiance appeared. It was an angel body made of light.*
> *Quartz and crystal, diamonds and coal, had become*
> *stars. Mineral consciousness had exploded into angelic*
> *consciousness.*

In retrospect now, I do not know what to make of these experiences. At times, I think that the shock of grief and the descent into mourning brought me back not only to my own beginnings, but also, perhaps, to the beginning. I wonder now if grief and mourning are not only a personal dying and being born, but also a dying and being born which find their resonance in these experiences and images of cosmic endings and beginnings. I wonder if in loss everything in us and about us that is personal is dissolved into something larger than ourselves. But I don't know. I only know that these experiences record some of the moments of mourning as I lived through them. And I know that others have left a similar record. Long ago, for example, the Persian poet Rumi placed death within the process of transformation from mineral to angel:

> I died to the mineral state and became a plant
> I died to the vegetative state and became an animal.
> I died there and became human. What have I ever

lost by dying? When was I less after a death?
When I shall bow down and die to being human, I
will lift my head to wake among the angels, and
I will move on from there as well! [9]

Rumi's words describe our many deaths, and while they imply some notion of progress in these dyings, a movement of ascent from stone to angel, nothing really prohibits us from saying that the angel lies as much on the near side of the mineral body as it does on the far side of it. Maybe, as the old Greek philosopher Heraclitus knew, the way up is the way down, and maybe the angel is the underside of the mineral body, those flecks of light released from shattered quartz, crystal, and diamond, dispersed throughout the cosmos as radiant points of energy, as stars. Maybe the angel is as deeply below us as it is above us, encountered in descent through the earth as it is in ascent toward the heavens. "One moment your life is a stone," the poet Rilke says, "and the next, a star."[10] Who knows? Maybe stones are weighted stars and stars lightened stones, heavenly jewels, angelic minerals. Maybe the heart hammered in grief releases our angelic light.

For a moment and only a moment, for an eternity and all eternity I rested there, on a pivot, on a threshold between worlds. The angel neither beckoned nor turned away. It neither welcomed nor rebuffed. All was balanced, in place, a perfect harmony of all creation. Perfect, total stillness.

Then the trembling began, an earthquake of the cosmic soul. Stars were falling from the sky. Deeper and deeper in the dark soil of earth, the shattered fragments of stone were coming together. Worm and mole were disgorging vegetable matter, and brown tubers were pushing through moist soil. A green shoot punctured the

> *skin of earth and celebrated the sun.*
>
> *It was morning. The landscape was empty, save for the vegetable womb watched over by the ancient, stone wizard. Womb and wizard were being warmed by the sun. The greenness of the vegetable cocoon was in shiny, wet abundance. I woke up and knew this was more than a dream.*

Gaston Bachelard has noted that "Melting into the basic element is a necessary human suicide for whoever wants to experience an emergence into a new cosmos."[11] My grief and mourning were a dying that opened into new life. They were a terrible passage through which I was forced to become more than what I was, where my consciousness was exploded beyond its human horizons.

We are at an evolutionary point in history where the one great task of exploration is the nature of consciousness. For whatever reasons on the part of creation, the human mind seems to be the sensitive receiver of the multiple and varied vibrations of consciousness which comprise the universe. We are the self-reflective part of creation, the agent through which the consciousness of creation continuously realizes itself. The telescopes through which we gaze at the stars are also the stars' way of looking at themselves. In this regard, the telescope, like all the instruments of technology, is a work of transformation.

In his poetry, Rilke was describing this work of transformation within another context. Commenting on his *Duino Elegies*, he claimed that words of lamentation and praise introduce "new frequencies into the vibration-spheres of the universe. Since the various elements in the cosmos are merely different rates of vibration," he added, "we are preparing in this way not only new intensities of a spiritual sort, but, who knows, new substances, metals, nebulae and stars."[12] There were times when the canopy of the starry night did seem like a blanket woven from my grief, and there were times when only this wide expanse of the starlit night seemed capable of containing my tears.

The physicist Itzhak Bentov situates consciousness in a similar way, which demonstrates how mind belongs to nature. Since the early part of this century, we have known from quantum theory that the mind of the experimenter is an integral factor in the experiment. The consciousness of the experimenter and the consciousness of subatomic particles interact. Of course, we are not used to speaking of the consciousness of matter, but that is only because we have isolated ourselves in the terribly lonely prisons of our own minds and have arbitrarily limited the notion of consciousness to the human domain. Only when this mind is shattered, as it is in grief or love, for example, do we know otherwise; or only when its familiar ways of thinking are challenged, as they were by quantum theory, do we broaden our vision.

In his work, Bentov argues for a spectrum or band of frequencies which differentiate types of consciousness from atoms through humanity to other spiritual realities (such as angels). Consciousness is frequency vibrations, a matter of harmonics, and consequently it consists of the capacity to be attuned to the environment and resonate with other and different harmonies. In this respect, vegetable consciousness compared with our consciousness, greenness compared with mind, is just another kind of energy whose frequency range overlaps with but is not identical to ours. Bentov has, in fact, diagrammed a series of energy exchange curves which illustrate this overlap among different frequencies of consciousness, different realities, and different levels of being. His point is that we experience something of vegetable consciousness on one side and angelic consciousness on the other side of our own minds.

But one does not really need these diagrams to recognize that the mind fragmented in grief, and lost in mourning, attests to these connections. Or at least we do not need them as factual proof, because the heart and soul of grief already know what the mind needs to prove.

It is best, then, to take these diagrams as stories, alongside others that are told by poet and painter, lover and mourner. Each in its own way declares that vegetable, animal, and even mineral consciousness interacts with us, just as angels and other orders of being touch us.

In my grief and mourning I felt as if I were on a path which led me to a communion with the consciousness of all creation, a path where traffic flowed in both directions. In my grief and mourning, I was opened to other vibrations of consciousness, other realities and the energies of other beings. And they opened themselves to me. Bentov makes this same point with respect to the dream. The animals we encounter in our dreams, he says, indicate "that they do reach into [our] level of consciousness."[13] Bentov is not saying that we dream the animal, nor is he saying the animal dreams us. Rather he is saying that dreams are the place where our consciousness and that of animals meet. So too are grief and mourning. They are the wild, winter landscapes where the world of green and stone, animal and angel, meet us.

Grief and mourning are the wilderness of the soul where we encounter the wild forces of nature. I think that what Bentov says of dreams also applies to grief and mourning, for each undoes the conscious mind. He notes that "what nature is doing to us during sleep (when we dream) is simply giving us a '"preview of coming events.'"[14] Might dreaming be considered nature's nightly way of preparing us for that expansive opening of mind which allows us to be in harmony with and to participate in the consciousness of all creation? And might grief and mourning do the very same thing? Might they not also be ways in which the narrow confines of our closed minds and fearful hearts are exploded and hurled into the stars?

The shock of grief and the slow, insistent process of mourning awakened me to the realization that the 'I' of my consciousness swims within a much wider and deeper sea of all creation. So there are times now when this 'I' whom 'I' am knows that the stones which I pass are dreaming of animals and angels, just as plants are dreaming of rocks and of us. And there are times too when I know that plants weep for the stony part of themselves they have left behind, just as angels weep for the flesh which we are. In such moments, it does seem to me that creation is a circuit of love and sorrow.

There are days now when so much of this seems of a different time and place, days too when I miss the quickened life of the world of green, the peace and stillness of the stone, and the awe-ful presence of the Angel. There are, however, no doorways into these kingdoms, at least none that we have built or to which our will is the key. We can, I think, only be open to these possibilities, open to those moments, for example, when some terrible loss pounds us into dust or when some unexpected love sweeps us off our feet, and we find ourselves in a place where the heart rules and the mind disappears. However it happens, we sense in such moments that we truly are part of a larger order, and for a moment, perhaps, we realize that without the pulsing rhythms of these other worlds, all our words are but empty abstractions, hollow husks, merely ideas about experience without the tumescent ripeness of it.

So, Yes! I do miss the presence of these other worlds. Grief did crack open the hard shell of the conventional life I was living, a shell made mostly of the unrecognized fear of losing not only what I loved but also what I had, and mourning did expand the horizons of my life. And yet, having lost once the one I truly but imperfectly loved, I would not choose to go into this place again. It will, of course, happen, because a life which embraces love, especially without too much fear, is and will be about loss. It will happen to me, and it will happen too to the one I love now most truly and fiercely, the one who, unknown to me, was waiting for me on the other side of mourning, and who loves me. I pray only that we will be able to know in those moments that there has been nothing left undone between us, no words left unspoken, no appeals left unwitnessed. And I pray that in those inevitable moments of sorrow the Green Man comes with all its force, the Mineral Wizard with all its patience, and the Angel with all its power. I pray that they all come in whatever guise each of us can receive them.

Beyond these speculations I would prefer to make nothing more of these reveries from the winter country of mourning. On the contrary, I prefer to let them stand as they are, as accounts simply of what happened, as stories which may or may not resonate with the experiences of others who have fallen out of the human world in grief and mourning. The task which these moments lay before us is, I now believe, that we be as faithful as we can to the experience as it happened, leaving to others their own responses. There really are no maps in these regions, and I would feel it a violation of the experience to make one for it now. So let all this be as it was, and let it all be as it is: the record of one witness whose grief and mourning shattered a human mind and opened an archaic, prehuman world where, by grace and love, it was healed.

CHAPTER

4

Mourning and Melancholy: The Orphan and the Angel

> Who's turned us round like this, so that we always,
> do what we may, retain the attitude
> of someone who's departing? Just as he,
> on the last hill, that shows him all his valley
> for the last time, will turn and stop and linger,
> we live our lives, for ever taking leave.
>
> **~*Rainer Maria Rilke***

FINAL MOMENTS ~

This image of the man on the hill, who, for the last time surveys his valley, who for a moment, one final moment, stops and turns and lingers, stirs the depths of the soul before it touches the surface of the mind. In everyone's life there are always these last moments, ones which mercifully each of us most often lives through without awareness of their finality. I was so fortunate—less than fifteen minutes before she died, I took my wife's face in my hands and told her how beautiful she was. If I knew that these minutes were to be our final ones, what would I have done? Even now I cannot think of it, because there would have been nothing I could have done to stop her dying.

We are nothing in the face of death except this: two lovers folded in each other's arms. That is all that nature grants us, but what a gift it really is. Sometimes, now, I imagine that there was a moment when the gods and goddesses of creation offered us this: the gift of love, provided we accept the fact of knowing we will die. Would any of us refuse the offer? Would we choose to live a life without love to remain ignorant of death? Even in the early moments of my grief, I never hated the bargain. Even in the midst of the pain of loss, I welcomed the fact that we had had twenty-five years of learning to be lovers. I only wished we had had more.

Forever taking leave, always on the verge of departing, we wander the world and along the way, at one time or another, meet others and, together for a brief moment, arrange things. We fall in love, marry, raise a family, start work, become knitted into the fabric of a community. Yet all the while we see with a deeper, third eye, a subtle erosion of all that we have so patiently and lovingly built. One by one the things we make slip away. One by one those whom we love pass on. And always in the dark silence of the night we know. Always in that deep hour of solitude we understand that death will take away the ones we love.

But where do they go, those whom we have loved and who have died? We soothe our children with stories of heaven, and even as adults we still continue to cherish this place in our hearts, even if we can no longer believe it with our minds. Something in us needs these tales. Something in us needs to imagine that love does endure, perhaps even beyond death. And yet, these stories can cheat us of the deepest demand which love makes upon us: to love what does not last, to love the rose which in its blooming already fades. To embrace here with love what will pass away, what is in this very moment passing, while still hoping for a love which lasts beyond the grave! How can we do that? Again, I don't know. I know only that after the shocks of grief and the long, slow winter of mourning, I have found myself experiencing the world through different eyes, as if grief and mourning had changed the prescription of my vision. In these moments, I experience all that is around me with melancholic eyes, with those eyes which can see in the midst of what is present in the moment, an absence which already haunts the moment. Melancholy, I now believe, is the mood which allows us to love in the midst of our continual dying. It is the mood which nurses the fact that love is born and rests in the cradle of death. It is the mood which allows us to bear the mystery of love as the fragile home which the homeless soul builds in the human heart.

CROSSING TO THE LIGHT

Sometime ago I took a drive with a colleague along the rugged Oregon coastline. Quite unexpectedly we encountered an invitation, a sign on the side of the road, that said "Sea Lion Cave," so many miles ahead. It was raining and cloudy, as it had been for the four or five days we had been in Oregon, and it seemed like a good idea to have a destination.

The entrance to the cave had a series of long, winding stairs leading to an elevator, which descended the last three hundred feet or so into the depths of the cave. The day was already quite chilly and the wind, needle like in its sharpness, whipped our faces as we stood on the outside platform awaiting our descent. Low angry clouds hung close to the water, intensifying a growing feeling of isolation, as if this landscape was quieting the busy ways of the mind. Yet I was hardly prepared for the moment when the door of the elevator opened and we descended the final flights of stairs into the cave.

The sea lions were visible from above the hollowed-out inlet— females with their pups born from the last mating. We were viewing the largest rookery on the North American coastline, a deep, wide scar cut into the rocks by the perpetual thrashing of the ocean tides. No one knows how long this place has existed, but one could not escape the impression of a kind of patient force at work here, a force of wind and tide marked with the index of eternity. Layer upon layer of rock had been sculpted by these forces, and once our eyes became accustomed to the darkness, we saw that almost every inch of layered rock was pulsating and quivering, animated by the sea lion inhabitants. Even long before we saw these creatures we had heard their incessant, continuous barking—deep, throaty sounds which had shaped the cave, echoing and filling the air with a sense of perpetual, unending hunger. Here, in the descent to the bottom I could hear the insatiable hungers of the animal soul: barking, pounding, rhythmical crescendos of longing, crashing like the tides against the rocks and the darkness of an everlasting night, blind appetites knowing nothing but hunger and its urgencies. Animal flesh: appetitive, instinctual, voracious, and eternal—the terror of the dark and of blind, carnal hunger.

I stood there, mesmerized by the sound and lost within it. It was only in retrospect that I realized the power of this event and the enormity of its effect. What broke me away from this eternal sea of instinctual hungers was the dim ray of light that weakly, so very weakly, was struggling to enter the cave from a crack above. I was seized by this light and its feebleness, and in a strange way I knew that somehow I was that light in the midst of all that darkness, struggling with the darkness, and perhaps even against it. In that moment, with a feeling of awe, terror, and sadness, I also knew that it was that light that distanced me from those sea lions, that light which placed between me and them an unbridgeable gap, that light, which was—at that moment, and had been, once before in the dawn of human consciousness—the tremulous bridge we had crossed out of the blindness of those instinctual hungers, out of the darkness of the night.

It was time to leave. As I turned away from the sea lions, I noticed that their sounds had grown farther away. When I rode the elevator up to the surface, these words came to mind: "and already the knowing brutes are aware/that we don't feel very securely at home/within our interpreted world." [1]

These lines are from the poet Rilke, and they capture something of the depth of my sense of homelessness in the scheme of creation. Compared with the animal, we truly are not so securely at home in our constructed world, especially when the winds of some deep sorrow whistle through the cracks in the walls of meaning we build to deal with suffering, pain, absence, loss, grief. Regarded from the point of view of the animal, "those knowing brutes," this world often does seem a hollow home.

Often, in a mood of melancholy, I had a sense of having left something behind, and in those moments the currents of my own personal grief were mixed with some larger grief, which I have come to associate with the figure of the Orphan. In melancholy the Orphan was my constant companion. More than that, I was seeing the world through the Orphan's eyes. Was my wife still somewhere in the world, perhaps just around that corner, waiting for my return? In melancholy my life took on this searching quality, as if everything and everyone held some secret, which, if I could divine it, would bring me home. I was, in these moments, also living my life with a backwards glance, like that man on the hill surveying his home for a last time. A simple gesture, this backward glance, and yet it seemed suffused with ancient rhythms. Did we once really cross to the light and leave behind something of ourselves, some archaic remnant which still dwells deep within our souls and is reborn in moments of loss and sorrow? Rilke again captures this old wound of longing borne by the Orphan in our souls:

> And yet, within the wakefully-warm beast
> there lies the weight and care of a great sadness.
> For that which often overwhelms us clings
> to him as well,—a kind of memory
> that what we're pressing after now was once
> nearer and truer and attached to us
> with infinite tenderness. Here all is distance,
> there it was breath. Compared with that first home
> the second seems ambiguous and draughty.
> Oh bliss of *tiny* creatures that *remain*
> for ever in the womb that brought them forth!
> Joy of the gnat, that can still leap *within*,
> even on its wedding-day: For womb is all."[2]

Was the sadness I felt in these moods of melancholy, that bittersweet taste, that mixture of sorrow and peace after the shocks of grief had passed and the winter storms of mourning had abated, if not ceased, the presence of the Orphan? Was the poet right? Was my own grief now being dissolved within this larger loss of a kinship we all once shared with the animal world? If I tell you that there were times when I saw a smile of recognition on the face of a cat and that these brief moments calmed me, would you believe me? Could you? In those moments, my heart knew that "these wakefully warm beasts" understood my sorrow. And my heart also knew that the sadness of those knowing brutes was in dim memory of our departure when we crossed into the light, sorrow for our folly, for the way in which we now must continually press after something which once, perhaps in the early morning of the world, was nearer and truer and already attached to us with an infinite tenderness. When I left the cave I felt sure that the animal marks with its sadness our loss of home, longs for our return, bears witness for a kinship we once shared but then sacrificed when we followed the light. I felt sure that the animal awaits and desires our homecoming.

I do not know why in melancholy I was so calmed by the presence of animals. Perhaps it was because of their simplicity, because, as Rilke implies, they are less burdened than we are by the weight of consciousness. I only know that in melancholy the weight of consciousness is lessened. In melancholy, you see the world through a veil of tears and through those tears the great round of life, love, and loss embraces you. In these moments, the mood of melancholy becomes the common bond which ties you to the fabric of all creation.

I am not suggesting here that melancholy erases the pain and grief of personal loss. My wife did die, and she is gone, forever, from this time and space. That plain fact, even to this day, still saddens me, and at times still overwhelms me. But I am saying that in melancholy her absence becomes part of a larger story. In melancholic moments, I can see her everywhere. She is in the dying of the light at the close of day, as well as in the rising of the sun at dawn. She is in the rain and in the seasons, in the changing of the leaves and the falling of the snow. In a curious way, then, her absence is not total. Now she belongs to all life. She is present everywhere. There is a strange peace granted by this vision, a paradoxical mix of sorrow and joy, which releases me back into life.

Perhaps, then, the appeal which animals have for us in our moments of sorrow is that they call us back to some earlier sense of home. In their presence, they seem to remind us that while we have lost our way the rest of creation waits our return.

THE GESTURE OF CONNECTION

It was a dark winter day when I made a visit to the Central Park Zoo in New York City. Winter days, particularly in midweek, have always been the best moments for zoo visits, as they afford solitude and private time with the animal.

On this occasion I was going to see the gorillas. Standing in front of the cage of a large silver back male, I keenly felt the presence of the bars between us. The gorilla was sitting in the front corner of his cage, and I could see him only in profile. On occasion, however, (as gorillas will do with zoo visitors) he would turn his head for a quick glance in my direction. His deeply set dark-black eyes seemed like pools of time, and in those few brief moments of exchange I felt dizzy, as if I could swim through his eyes into another world. But the gorilla would just as quickly look away, and the spell would be broken. The cage was so small, especially for so large an animal, and I wondered how he could bear it. His lethargy was inescapable, and I thought of the many hours of boredom he must daily endure, wondering, too, if I was reading my own sense of melancholy through him. But I had also been with animals in the wild, and the difference in behavior, in gesture, and in that imaginal space between us was pronounced. Caught up in these reveries, I had absentmindedly withdrawn an orange from my pocket and was tossing it in the air. The gorilla turned and began to watch me. Without thinking I tossed the orange through the bars to him, momentarily oblivious to the prohibition against feeding the animals. The toss of the orange through the bars covered a distance of only a few feet in real space and took perhaps only a second in real time. But the gesture, and what unexpectedly followed, bridged an ocean of time and space.

One would have expected the gorilla to take the orange and retreat to a far corner of the cage to eat it. But this gorilla did not. Instead, he tossed it through the bars back to me, I caught it, and in my astonishment, I tossed it to him again. We continued like this for perhaps three exchanges, until this ribbon between us, this embrace of a game, was broken by the sound of a voice from the far end of the corridor. "Don't feed the animals!" When I turned toward the voice, the gorilla turned away. He moved to the far end of the cage. He kept the orange.

I left the zoo and walked out into the city. The cold, dark, winter afternoon did little to cheer the sadness I felt at having left the gorilla inside. I was different, changed by that encounter and even more lonely in the midst of the crowded city. The gorilla had suspended his appetite for a moment. For the sake of an encounter, he had bridged an immense gap between our worlds. In his gesture of tossing the orange back to me, he had reached out his hand across an emptiness so vast as to be beyond measure. Together we had built a tremulous bridge of gestures, and for a brief time we stood on opposite sides of that bridge, connected in a way that seemed to acknowledge in each other a lost kinship. Even to this day, I know that I'll never forget the eyes of my winter companion on that day of long ago. He had greeted me, and as strange as it might sound, I felt so grateful for that recognition. But I also felt how far I had come, and I knew with a deep feeling of sadness that we would remain forever more on opposite sides of this bridge, and that at the best moments of my life, I would be able only to stop and linger and turn around to see, once again, what was left behind. I knew that, and I knew, too, that what I saw in his eyes before the spell was broken was his sadness for me.

I seem now to live in the world in this way, attuned to these connections, tied by some invisible threads to a sense of loss that seems to inhabit all things. When I wake in the morning, the songs of the birds fill me with a sad kind of peace, but I feel a strange gratefulness for these small gifts of creation. The smell of the flowers, the endurance of the mountains, and even the sound of the cool wind as it moves through the trees—all these really ordinary things strike a melancholic chord in my soul which connects me to the world. How else can I say it? These simple things are friends, companions, and in these moments of melancholy, when the winter storms of mourning have lessened, I feel welcomed by them. Indeed, the melancholy which has followed upon my grief seems at times like a homecoming. In this mood I feel like the orphan who is coming home.

THE ORPHAN ~

The Orphan is a kind of archetypal figure of the melancholic mood, an image for this moment of the grieving process which is more than personal, which has a shared, perhaps universal, quality to it. It is a kind of code of the soul by which strangers recognize each other as fellow travelers. It is a pattern in human experience for the deep longing to be home and for the awareness that we are always on the way, that home is as much a destiny which awaits us as it is a heritage which sustains us

To be an orphan, Saint Augustine says, relates one to God. Carl Jung's psychology of individuation makes a similar claim. For Jung this process of individuation is an ongoing incarnation of God for the sake of divine transformation. In becoming who we are called to be, we bring God into his creation. In this respect, it might be proper to say that the divine enters the world through the cracks in creation, including, and perhaps especially so, in our moments of breakdown and loss. Perhaps, then, the Orphan is our God-face, the face which we wear when loss cracks open our stony hearts into wider fields of love. In these moments, the Orphan is the one who is present to the holy splendor of the ordinary, the one who sees the miracle in the simplest moment, the one who glimpses the numinous quality in the shadows of loss. If anyone had tried to tell me that any of this would happen to me after my wife died, I could not have believed them. Now I cannot help but walk in the presence of the Orphan.

LOVE IN THE FACE OF LOSS

Once, long ago now, I stepped across a threshold into an ancient church. Gothic in design, and dating back to the fourteenth century, its interior gloom was matched by the heavy dampness and the chill which hung in the atmosphere. True, I was tired after a long day of walking in the hills around the city, but my own fatigue only made me more open and receptive to the heavy weight which fell upon my spirit in that cold, dark, and empty place. As I walked through the chapel I caught sight of a wooden beam near the altar. Even in the fading light of the day I could see that there was an inscription carved into the wood, written in fourteenth century English which made

*some of the words appear strange in their spelling. I was
drawn to it, as if to a magnet, witnessing what someone,
long ago, had inscribed:*

> "How low! how fleeting! are the joys of Earth
> How vain to build on hopes this side the Grave
> Full soon the Rose that blooms may fade by Death
> Beyond the powers of human skill to save"

*I have not forgotten these words from so long ago,
and occasionally they come back to me with a haunting
presence. They are certainly an admonition, probably
against pride and perhaps even a cry of despair, an
expression of hopeless resignation in the face of illness,
suffering, and death. But I am certain that these words
have lingered with me because they also signaled
something else. Without realizing it then, they wove into
the fabric of my being another thread. Even in the face of
illness, suffering, and death, someone, someone now so
long ago, spoke those words, carved them in wood, and
left them as a beacon, a sentinel to reach across time
and touch a weary traveler.*

*This message of so long ago is a beautiful paradox.
The words, in spite of their meaning on one level, open
toward a future, and in this opening they register a sense
of hope. Someone, whomever it was, did build on this
side the grave. Someone did speak, even in the presence
of that knowledge that the rose that now blooms will fade
by death.*

*In odd moments, most often when I am walking in
the hills alone, I like to think of that someone as a
companion, a fellow orphan. In these moments, I like to*

remember that weary traveler and whisper a word of thanks for leaving behind in the face of loss a message of love.

In accepting the responsibility of our orphanhood, we become faithful sentinels for the passing and the flowering of the world. The Animal perishes but we, and those whom we love, die. In this difference, that gesture where we turn, stop, look, and linger is born, that backwards glance which says, in effect, that as we move through life we know we are forever taking leave, leaving something behind, that awareness which recognizes that life truly is about building hopes this side the grave, loving in the face of loss. In a curious way, then, the Orphan, the most homeless of all, is the one who most appreciates the journey towards home, and who understands that this journey is marked by a fierce devotion to each moment as it presents itself.

Could I have loved my wife in this way when she lived, perhaps the winter of my mourning would have been less severe. But I did not. I failed, in large part, I think, not only because I was too afraid to love, too fearful of losing her, but also because I always thought we had more time, many more moments, a long stretch of tomorrows. But none of us is even promised the next moment, none of us even assured of the next breath. The Orphan knows this truth, and knowing it embraces each moment in its fullness. I remember now that last moment, when I saw the beauty on her face. How odd that at that moment, just before her fading, she was in the full bloom of her person. I had to lose the one I loved in order to appreciate that the rose is at its ripest moment of life when in its blooming it is already fading. I had to lose the one I loved, when what I really wanted was to grow old together.

FAILED DEDICATIONS

I had gathered her writings and photographs. My intention was to mark her passing with some kind of memorial. She had produced so much, and I wanted some trace of her to be left here, with all of us. I did not want her to be erased from the world, her spirit washed over by the ongoing tide of life, the waters closing over her and our memories of her. It was a duty, and I was desperate to say to the world that this woman had lived, that she had loved and been loved, and that she had left behind for us a record which commanded our attention. Others had to take notice, and with a furious energy I threw myself into multiple projects of dedication and remembrance.

In the midst of these efforts, I remembered the night I had spent in the hospital with my mother. She was nearly eighty years old at that time and was scheduled the next morning for quadruple bypass surgery. The odds were quite against her, and I knew, and I think that she knew, that this evening might very well be our last. We talked for a while, but mostly she just wanted to hold my hand.

As morning approached she fell into a restful sleep, and when the dawn came, I went out into the street. The cool morning air felt refreshing against my face. As I walked the streets, my mother was being wheeled into surgery. The city was slowly coming to life, and in the midst of the increasing activity I felt a strange sense of alienation from my surroundings. No one knew of the struggle that my mother was undergoing at that moment. I wanted to shout out what was happening, that a woman's life might be coming to a close inside the walls of that hospital. I could see the whole span of my mother's life, an arc stretching from her youth to this moment of her old age, and I wanted the others in the street whom I passed, all of them strangers, to take notice that a human life might be passing from this world. But they all seemed so very far away, and I felt like a visitor to some foreign land. She would pass away, and no one would notice.

I struggled against this memory, fought hard against its presence in this moment of dedications. I would make others listen, make them attend to the passing of my wife. I swore with a kind of crazed energy that I would not let her sink into the waters of oblivion. But I failed. In the end, out of sheer exhaustion, I stopped these projects of dedication. I packed the albums away, stored the articles, and placed all of it in a trunk.

I realize now, however, that it is this work which is the dedication. Not a monument, constructed of the articles of her life, not a museum of sorts, but closer to a living testimony which does not simply remember our love, but also goes on loving in expressing the quiet sense of joy and the simple sense of peace which has arisen from grief and mourning. For what do the dead want from us? A sacrifice of our lives? No! I think they ask of us to go on celebrating the rhythms of life, but now in a special way. I think they ask us to become better lovers by taking notice of the dying which belongs to all life, and in the midst of this raise our voices in songs of praise. This is what the Orphan can do: sing those hymns of praise and joy which flower from lament and loss.

Some years ago now, in a book entitled *Technology as Symptom and Dream*, I argued that the threat of nuclear holocaust needs to move us beyond fear of the future into grief in the present for the loss of all that surrounds us and matters to us.[3] Little did I realize then that it would be my own personal grief which would move me into that place where the figure of the Orphan would awaken me to the dying of creation and open my heart to the necessities of and requirements to love. Now more than ever, I wonder if we have become so estranged from the world that we no longer are moved by the suffering of the trees, the sorrow of the animals, the sadness of the stars? Is it only now our own personal sorrows which touch us? Have we become so distant, so remote, so removed from the rest of creation, that we are no longer able to respond to the simple appeal of things? And then, unable to respond, have we become irresponsible, careless, neglectful, and even destructive? The poet Rilke understood this simplicity of things, and the appeal they lay before us:

> "These things that live on departure
> understand when you praise them: fleeting, they look for
> rescue through something in us, the most fleeting of all."[4]

To awaken to the Orphan in our grief is the necessary precondition for hearing the lament of the world, for witnessing its dying, and perhaps, if we are lucky, assisting in its healing. Today we desperately need a transformation of soul, a radical spiritual revolution. The Orphan who arises in our souls from the ashes of our grief is one step in this transformation.

Earlier I said that to be an orphan relates one to God. In this regard, the Orphan is also the figure of our souls who, although most homeless, beckons us toward our spiritual home. Here, I believe the Orphan encounters the Angel. Why the Orphan and the Angel dwell together, I do not really know. But sometimes I feel that they hold between them the tension of home and homelessness, which seems to lie at the root of the soul. Noel Cobb, poet and Jungian analyst, says it this way: "Angels above us, around us and below us—/ Did you not have to become outcasts/ In order to discover your true home?"[5]

Angels as outcasts; orphans as angels! Is the Angel a piece of us left behind, the Orphan part of ourselves? Is the Orphan in the soul a kind of spiritual deposit of our angelic existence, a residue of that part of ourselves left behind to remind us from where we come and where we are going? I think sometimes of my Orphan companion as bits of angel dust left in the soul. At other times, it feels as if the Angel's wing is lightly dusting the Orphan's cheek, and in these moments I sense a connection between them, a kinship outside my ordinary experiences of time and space. In a moment like this, it seems to me that the mood of melancholy, which attends the Orphan's presence, could be the aftertaste of our angelic existence, or a foretaste of it, or perhaps a bit of both—a heritage and a destiny. But, again, I do not know. I know only that my grief, mourning, and the passage into melancholy opened a path in my life where these questions now seem quite vital to me.

But who and what is the Angel who, as counterpart to the Orphan, draws us beyond ourselves, transforming our sorrow? Such a question belongs to the province of the human heart and always lies on the far side of either factual proof or logical reason. The Angel often comes in a moment of oblique vision, when the human eye has softened its gaze, when the Orphan in his or her solitude regards the world with a melancholic vision. Now I wonder if the Orphan is the Angel's way of tapping us on the shoulder, perhaps initiating that backwards glance. In such a moment, the Angel might appear.

THE ANGEL ~

SO FIERCE ITS STREAMING BEAUTY

The stillness was so deeply impressive—a kind of stillness I had felt only once before, in Africa—the stillness of the early morning of the world, before "we" came. It was not that I was aware of the silence. Rather, the silence was already there, wrapped within itself, complete, fulfilled, without need of sound. This silence was its own consciousness, aware of itself as a slow, rhythmic, vaporous liquidity, the mist of the early morning of the world, floating, condensing, dissolving, congealing in a sleepy kind of dumbness. And the light–soft, yellow-white, spreading itself with the mist, textured, palpable, diaphanous, the veil of the world's first morning, gathering itself, and in the next moment an epiphany. Formed out of nothing but this light, a being so composed within itself, so tranquil, unstirred by the mist; calm, serene, beatific. A being so beautiful, before distinctions, neither male nor female in form nor young nor old in face, neither conscious nor unconscious, neither awake nor asleep. Creation's first image before time, eternal, unmoved, so peaceful in its splendid indifference. Creation itself, complete! Once, now long ago, I said of such a being: 'So fierce its streaming beauty, so terrible its averted gaze!'⁶ The Angel: mirror of our failure, measure of our loss?

"Every angel is terrible," Rilke says, acknowledging those moments of mystery when the veils of perception lift from our eyes and we stand motionless for a small, brief moment between two worlds. The terrible angel is an earthquake of the soul, a tear in the fabric of space and time, and also a miracle. Rilke addresses angels as "almost deadly birds of the soul," "early successes, creation's pampered darlings." They are "dawn red ridges of all beginning, —pollen of blossoming Godhead," emptying or exploding like seeds out of the center of creation, cascading and tumbling into the corridors of time to germinate in the recessed chambers of the human heart. "Hinges of light," he calls them, shining pivots of energy, shimmering, resonating, vibrating at frequencies which we, with our poor consciousness, can tune into with only just enough awareness to be filled with longing. "Shields of felicity, tumults of stormily-rapturous feeling and suddenly, separate," the angel is aloof, withdrawn, nearly beyond the boundaries of our gaze, and even indifferent to our presence. Angels are "mirrors, drawing up their own outstretched beauty into their faces again."[7] In sacred literature we are told that you are struck dumb when you meet such an angel. Yes! So fierce its streaming beauty, and so terrible its averted gaze!

Who is the Angel? Blaise Pascal, seventeenth-century philosopher, mathematician, and polymath, looking into the endless depths of the heavens, felt the acute loneliness of our human condition and the anxiety that accompanies the recognition of the vast emptiness that engulfs our mortal lives. So many times after my wife died I felt Pascal's anxiety. Those vast spaces seemed to me an index or measure of my own feeling of loss: my feeling of no longer being at home or of having any sense of home. But I was also drawn to that infinite expanse, because its deep blackness was ancient and more than human. In that archaic, cosmic space, I could lose my own personal sorrow, and within that space the splendid indifference of the Angel seemed the right mirror for the anonymity which I sought.

This question about the Angel is a matter of the human heart, and such matters always lie on the far side of reason. Pascal knew this as well. In the deep recesses of the human heart, he found that the "heart has its reasons which reason itself does not know."[8] When my heart cracked in grief, an angel appeared. But how do I speak of any of this? Words which follow the heart are quite different and more difficult than those which come from the mind. "Tell all the Truth," the poet Emily Dickinson enjoins us, "but tell it slant."[9] That seems sound advice when trying to speak of the Angel. In this realm nothing is certain, and everything that I feel I can say could also be said in the opposite way. Perhaps that is why there is a hierarchy in the choir of angels. Maybe those angels who are closest to God are closest to home and, therefore, farthest from us and so indifferent to us, while those nearer to us appear in a different way. That splendid indifference described above, for example, contrasts sharply with the Angel who beckons and guides us home.

THE HILL ABOVE THE CITY

The day was snowy and the forecast promised continuous snow. I was determined, however, to drive the mountain roads toward Pikes Peak. In the year or so since my wife had died, I was still possessed with feelings of having to prove my right to go on living. Risks like this one were dares thrown out to the universe. I was pitting my will against something other, some invisible force in creation, which I blamed for my wife's death, something anonymous against which I felt only a terrible rage. I would force it to declare itself, challenging it to take me, like it had stolen my wife.

As I drove up the mountain, the weather turned more cold and gray. The snow was now falling in heavy clusters, whipped by the wind into frenzied currents which blocked my vision. But I refused to turn back, and I continued to plow my way along the icy road. As I neared the top, I felt a fevered giddiness, and I had the strange sense that at the summit I would pass into a cloud of whiteness and disappear into another realm. Not into death exactly, but out of this time and space. I knew too that she was there, a figure clothed in white, waiting for me in this cold, frozen place.

The gate at the park ranger's booth was down, and a sign clearly indicated that the road had been closed because of the weather. I left the car, and, standing at the gate, I felt that my life now hung in the balance. I could easily have walked around the gate and continued up the mountain, but I knew that if I did so I would die. Did I want to die? I turned around and looked down the road I had just traveled. Below me was the city, invisible now because of the heavy snow. I could not choose. But out of the stormy breath of the wind, I heard a voice: "Go back. You belong below, there in the city." It was a quiet voice, a gentle voice, the voice of my wife.

The landscape was reminiscent of a landscape in a dream I had a year earlier, shortly after my wife's death. The only difference was that in the dream my wife is standing on a green hill. She is shimmering like water does when it is rippled by a breeze on a soft summer day. I climbed the hill toward her, feeling a deep sense of happiness at having found her. She seemed so far away, however, and no matter how far I walked, I could not close the distance between us. And yet, despite the distance, I could see her face quite clearly. She was happy and at peace. I wanted to be with her, and I knew that she knew that. But she only smiled and without any other sign I also knew that I had to stop my journey toward her. That smile was filled with so much love, that even to this day, when I recall the dream, I can still feel its warmth.

I turned and looked back toward the city below the hill. It too seemed to glimmer, like a green jewel. I knew I was meant to return to it, that it was not yet my time to pass into that other place beyond this life.

Whether the Angel appears in the guise of splendid indifference or in warming compassion, its presence heralds a crack in our familiar world. In this sense, the poet Rilke is right when he says that every angel is terrible. Every angel is as terrible as a miracle, a strange testimony to the existence of other realms of being beyond our ordinary mortal concerns; moreover, because they are miracles, they are not at our command. They come in dreams or in visions or they break through in moments of breakdown. In his classic text, *A Handbook of Angels*, the physician H. C. Moolenburgh says that "angels always wait till the last possible moment."[10] They stand, as it were, at the edge of human events, or they wait, perhaps, in the very depths of our sorrows and distress.

So much of our talk about the angel today, however, seems either to forget or to disregard the radical otherness of the Angel. So much of it seems designed to bring the Angel into our human realm, so much of it filled with advice about channeling the angel, often at times with instructions on how to do so, as if there were, or even could be, a twelve-step program for evoking an angel. I do not mean, however, to dismiss these practices. I mean only to emphasize the radical difference of the Angel from us, to leave it in its holy and terrible splendor, to stand in awe before its otherness. Indeed, I believe that we are spiritually hungry for this sense of radical holy otherness, starving for something other to address the Orphan in us, to respond to the deep and growing sense of homelessness at the core of our broken hearts. It is this hunger, I believe, which fuels so much of our angel talk today. But we are also impatient, and so we unwittingly reinforce our spiritual starvation to the degree that we domesticate the Angel to our own needs and concerns.

When the Angel comes, it comes unbidden, and it is we who are addressed, called, challenged, changed. Despite our impressive technological powers, we can no more manage the Angel's appearance than we can engineer a miracle. We cannot even say the Angel is a symbol, because in its radical otherness the Angel lies beyond our understanding. To understand something or someone is to stand under it, to ground it, to give it our support. If anything, it is the other way around with the Angel. The Angel grounds us, gives us our place, marks the boundary, as it were, of our station between itself and the Animal, of which we are neither.

But we do, of course, symbolize the Angel. The great medieval paintings of the angels, with their dominant size and powerful wings, bless the eye. These symbols, however, barely touch the Angel. They allude to a presence beyond us which always remains elusive. When I look, for example, at da Vinci's *Annunciation*, those magnificent wings remind me that whatever and however angels might be, they do fly from our grasp and always escape our comprehension. Perhaps the medieval artist knew better than we do today that through the symbol we glimpse the invisible but we never possess it. Perhaps he knew that we must, therefore, always take our symbols lightly and that the truest moment of our symbols is their failure. The Angel is not the image. Nor is the Angel what I say in these poor words. The image and the word, at their best, only open a space where the Angel might appear.

Rilke, whose ten *Duino Elegies* are so devoted to the Angel, rightly regarded their elusive presence. Allowing himself at moments to hope otherwise, he asked, "Do the angels really/only catch up what is theirs, what has streamed from them, or at times, /as though through an oversight, is a little of our/existence in it as well?"[11] But Rilke knew better than to sustain that hope, and he knew too that against that hope the Angel remains quite beyond us. Thus for him the Angel always remained "terrible," terrible because for us who still depend so much upon the material, visible world, the Angel is "...that creature in which the transformation of the visible into invisibility appears already fulfilled."[12]

I understand what Rilke means here. Grief cracked the lineaments of my taken-for-granted world, the visible world of my everyday concerns, and through the cracks that other world of the invisible where angels dwell broke through. The effect was and continues to be that backwards glance with which I now regard this world, the city below the hill. This world is home and yet not home. In this strange paradox, there are moments when I feel I am seeing things as if for the last time, and I linger just a bit longer with them, grateful for their presence, attached to them with a new kind of tenderness and love.

SUNRISE

I woke early. It was still dark, but in the east the first ray of the morning sun was beginning to crack the shell of night. The camp was perhaps fifty yards from the river, and I made my way slowly down the unfamiliar path, stupidly oblivious to the danger of the animals in the African bush. The water was cold, but it sharpened my senses. Across the river, on the opposite bank, a range of hills framed the valley. As the sun gained in strength, the ridge of these hills was outlined in a thin, delicate purple line, as if someone had ribboned the top edge of them. The contrast between the dark hills, still shadowed in night, and their purple crown was beautiful, and as I stared at this artful display of nature, I saw what appeared to be stone statues carved into the hilltop. From the distance, I could not quite make out their form. But I was certain that they were made of stone because of their total stillness.

In one single moment, the sun broke the last vestige of night. Rising above the peak of the hills, it flooded the valley with light. And at the exact same moment of this epiphany, the stone statues came to life and filled the valley with sound. The stone carvings that I had seen just before the dawn were transformed into a troop of baboons, who were now screeching and moving in a kind of wild, ecstatic dance. I knew in an instant that in their previous frozen stillness they had been waiting for the morning sun, gathered like monks in prayer before the dawn.

I do not claim that there are angels in this story. But I do wonder if the morning sunrise is for these animals something like a miracle and, therefore, akin to our encounters with an Angel. Maybe each dawn is a miracle, and maybe we have just forgotten how to see it. And maybe the morning light is the radiance of the Angel filling the world, and we need to be reminded of it. I do not know. But I do claim that when my world was wrecked by grief and the Orphan was awakened, I became more attuned to the fact that I am orphaned between two worlds, between that of the Animal and that of the Angel, and that I am not fully at home in either one. In such a moment, my personal grief was enfolded within a larger, I might even say, cosmic story.

For whatever it is worth, I have found this realization to be comforting. In the heart of it I find a strange kind of peace and wisdom which persuades me that we pass beyond this life as part of our journey home. But I find too that the journey deeply matters and not just its end, and thus I find that I have a deeper attachment to the daily mysteries and miracles of this world, even to the point where I know at times that we are, in one respect, the envy even of angels.

Angels wish they had beards to enjoy the pleasure of the sound
Of scraping the passage of time from faces
Worn with sorrows, lighted with joys.
They wish too to sense the clarity of lemons
And to smell the scent of someone in love.
They want to hear a lover say,
'I will always tease your flesh.'
In their airy kingdoms beyond this world,
In their beautiful indifference,

In their silent stillness,
They dream, always, their own betrayals:
To grow old and ill, even to die, and to hear a lover say,
Even once, if only once,
I would rather lose you to another lover than to God.[13]

I wrote this poem a few months after my wife died. The last line
was one she had spoken to me several months before her death. I was
struck then by the forcefulness of her commitment to life. I am certain
now that, although she left life too soon, she did not leave without
having tasted deeply of its gifts and pleasures.

Somewhere in the mists of time there was a moment when a shaft
of weak light pierced the dark cave of life, when a spark ignited between
Animal and Angel, and the Orphan was born. In the melancholy that
comes after grief, I have often felt that we are the continuance of that
moment, a small flame that lights the way toward creation's continuing
evolution, the arc that connects matter and spirit, the pivot around
which Animal and Angel dance, creatures who, when we gaze in the
mirror, glimpse two faces and who remember the early morning of
the world when angel and animal were one, and who now are
continually called to bring that first morning into tomorrow. Between
that first morning and tomorrow we are asked to endure, to live our
lives, to bear our burdens, to love our families, to bury the dead. It is
so difficult a place to be, yet it is the only place we have. Rilke says,

Between the hammers lives on
our heart, as between the teeth
the tongue, which, nevertheless,
remains the bestower of praise.[14]

Such a fine image: the soft tongue set between hard teeth continues
to praise. Grief has been a radical transformation of my life, and the
long, slow winter of mourning has been a prelude to a spiritual
awakening. In the midst of my sorrow, I was always so much less than

what I would be, but also so much more than what I once was. And now when I look into the faces of those whom I love, I see mirrored back to me the face of the Orphan, and I stop for a moment and I linger before I take my leave.

PART THREE

LYRICAL IMPROVISATIONS
IN CELEBRATION OF THE WORLD

There are many other kinds of consciousness
in the cosmos besides human consciousness

~ Matthew Fox and Rupert Sheldrake

CHAPTER

5

The Spider's Web, the Bird's Song,
and the Ballet of the Whale

THE ANATOMY THEATER~

Mors ubi gaudet succurrere vitae

These words are carved into the doorway of the anatomy theater at the University of Padua in Italy. It is one of the oldest anatomy theaters in Europe, and one of the first places where our modern sciences of anatomy and physiology were born. Years ago, I had written of this place and the early pioneers of medicine who labored there, but before this visit I had never been there, and I did not know of this inscription. It shocked me, and I struggled with my rusty Latin to decipher its meaning. I knew the individual words, but the ensemble did not make sense. Specifically, the word *succerrere* puzzled me. "Where death rejoices to run under life," was the literal translation, but somehow that seemed wrong, or not quite in the spirit of the place.

For me *succerrere* as "to run under" evoked images of blood draining from a dead body lying on a dissecting table. An intolerable image which immediately resurrected the image of my wife lying on the emergency room table after she had died. Five years had already passed since that time, but in the anatomy theater the image of her on the emergency room table was haunting the edges of the dissecting table. I saw her hair, already so limp, so lacking in life and I turned away from what I saw—that was not her. It was not even her dead body, but something less than that, an object, a thing, something foreign, strange, even beyond death—a corpse.

In the five years since my wife's death, grief had taught me how the time of the soul differs from the time of our waking ego-consciousness, the time of mind. For the soul, moments in time are not arranged on a horizontal line, like beads on a string. The past is not what has happened and is over; nor is the future what is about to happen. For the soul, moments in time have a vertical depth, and moments, which for the ego-mind are separated into past, present, and future, are drawn together by an affinity of mood and image. A magnetic or gravitational pull seems to exist among these moments, which dissolves the linear quality of time.

My experience in the anatomy theater was not a memory of something which happened five years earlier. To interpret it in this way would betray the fact that right there in the anatomy theater I was living that moment in the hospital for the first time. Indeed, I was not able to tuck safely away in the past the intolerable image of that thing on the emergency room table, the corpse which was an obscene caricature of my wife. That intolerable image had scratched its way into my soul, and was waiting there for the moment when it could present itself again to me, when it could make use of another occasion to take hold of me, and penetrate to the core of my being. The anatomy theater offered that occasion.

For a long time I was shaken by the immediacy of this experience. When, however, the intolerable image began to fade, I became aware that something else was at work in this situation. Beyond the intolerable image, death wanted to tell me something more. The theater became crowded with the ghosts of all those early pioneers who had labored over the dead in search of knowledge. Where death rejoices they whispered. Suddenly, I understood. In this place where the human body as an anatomical specimen was born nearly five centuries ago, death had not yet irrevocably parted company with life. Death had not yet been made into the enemy. "Where death rejoices to be in support of life"—that is what the inscription meant. A subtle difference in that single word—*succerrere*—but a world of difference between a corpse on a dissecting table from which blood has been drained away, or a table in an emergency room, and a dead body around which there still lingers the spirit of the one who was loved and who has died.

Something of this difference had already been present in those first moments in the hospital. After I had left the room, I realized that my wife's rings were still on her finger. I panicked. The feeling that the body on the table, was not her returned, and I knew I had to rescue the rings for her and myself, those rings stolen by death. But I could not face that obscene caricature of my wife's body again. I could not go back into that room, and certainly I could not touch what was no longer her hand. At that moment I asked of a friend what, in retrospect, I have come to realize was an almost impossible task. I asked him to enter that room and remove the rings.

Over the years I have come to appreciate what a supreme act of courage and love he performed for me and my wife at that moment. In that early shock of loss, he had already made a place for love. Only recently, after reading these words, did he tell me that when he saw my wife in the emergency room she was still enveloped in the beauty, eros, and vitality of her living presence. How I wish now I could have been with my wife in that moment in that way, that I too could have been a witness to the still present force of her beautiful life. But I could not. I could not do it then. Nor was I ever able to return to that moment in memory. The corpse was an intolerable image, a frozen emptiness, and that moment in the emergency room a blank space in my soul.

But while I was unable to return in memory to that moment in time, I was returned to it during this visit to the anatomy theater. And I was returned, I believe, because that emergency room moment and its intolerable image needed and wanted to be witnessed. What we turn away from haunts us. Moments in the time of the soul wait for us as occasions in the world. They wait for us to be ready. In the hospital I was not ready.

I can, of course, explain my reaction in the hospital as a case of shock, but that after all is only a word which needs a context. The truth is that the death of my wife, which was so quick and so completely unexpected, overwhelmed me with the horrible finality of death. The shift from her living presence to the mannequin-like corpse was too swift.

For me, the rituals of death only continued this too-quick transformation of the dead body of my wife into a corpse, into an alien and foreign thing, and I had little chance to say good-bye in a proper way. The professionalization of death stole her body away from me and its surroundings; the funeral parlor replaced the parlor at home. Taken from its familiar place, the dead body of my wife became unrecognizable. In fact, when I first saw her at the funeral parlor, before anyone else had been ushered into the room, she was so unlike who she was in life that I insisted on a closed coffin. She was not there, in that tomb of flesh, and I hated the mockery represented by that frozen image of her. I thought it a cruel and mean illusion which asked us to pretend that who she was could be identified with that cold, doll-like thing in the box.

But, then, where was she now? Certainly, she was dwelling in the conversations which were whispered among the mourners. She was not in that box, not present in that literal way; she was in our hearts, already in that other imaginal landscape of the soul, in the stories which were being spoken, and in the tears which were being shed. How curious it was to me to see how often those stories told of her were accompanied by a soft smile on the face of the speaker, as if the telling itself was somehow also a small moment of joy. Here in the stories told among the living, it seemed to me that death was already in support of life.

So many times I have wondered what my wife's death asks of me and what she too asks, and so many times has the reply been to go on living. But even to say it this way is not enough, because it fails to capture the sense of joy for life, of rejoicing in living, which can arise, and for me has arisen, after the long winter of mourning. Simple pleasures, like the song of a bird, that once went unnoticed take on a special, at times even numinous quality, and there is something like a lyrical appreciation for the small and tiny miracles of the everyday world. In this sense, I do think that death can be in support of life and that there can arise from grief a birth into a wider, and somewhat freer, field of life and love.

Earlier in this book, I said how much the poets meant to me in the early moments of my grief and especially in the long winter of its mourning. They were the best companions, I believe, because they address the soul's grief in an immediate way and not the mind's need to do something about it. We are so good at the latter, and so poor at the former that we hunger for those tiny moments of rescue, when we can surrender ourselves to the rhythms of the soul, when we can let go of managing our sorrows and allow ourselves to be led and transformed by them.

And so, again, I am not surprised that it is a poet who understands this strange blend of death and joy. Writing of this mysterious marriage, Rilke says,

Only in the realm of praising may Lament go.[1]

These words belong to his *Sonnets to Orpheus*, sonnets to that tragic figure of myth who persuaded the gods and goddesses of the underworld to release his beloved dead wife, Eurydice. As I said earlier, they were so moved by his song of lament that they granted him his wish on condition that he not look back as he exited their realm. But he failed in the last moment, and, fearful that she was not behind him, he turned and forever lost her to death. Grievous beyond solace, he wandered the world in mourning, so oblivious to all appeals to love again that he was finally killed by the women of Thrace who, in their frenzied jealousy, became the Maenads who tore Orpheus to pieces. As the story goes, his body parts were thrown into the sea, where, some say, they were retrieved and buried by the Muse of song, while his head and lyre eventually landed on the island of Lesbos, a place devoted to the sacred mysteries of love. There his head continued to sing its songs, and eventually his lyre was hurled into the heavens, where it now rests as a constellation of stars.

Like all myths, this story recounts the wisdom of the soul which holds a connection among love, death, lament, song, and even the stars. I know that for myself there has been this unexpected connection between grief and the stars, and while I can offer no rational explanation for it, I can swear that the starry night does belong to the soul in grief, as if that wide expanse is its home. So I find comfort in Rilke's words when he says that Orpheus, that figure "appointed to praising," is the one whose song "came like the ore forth from the stone's silence."[2] The stone's silence, like that mineral consciousness below green which I described earlier, is the hard and long endurance of lament. But, like Orpheus' tale, lament bursts forth beyond the stony stillness of grieving to sing the stars. The destiny of sorrow seems to be a journey from stony silence to starry constellation. The range of lament seems to be from grief endured to a hymn of praise for all creation. For the soul, if not the mind, lament and praise belong together, stony silence and stellar song. For the soul, if not the mind, it seems right to say,

Only one who has lifted the lyre
among shadows too,
may divining render
the infinite praise.[3]

Grief and mourning are not only psychological conditions. They are also cosmological opportunities. When out of lament we praise the world, we release those things that we praise into their larger domain, and with their release we win our own, as well as the release of the one who has died. Why is it that the soul in grief can eventually begin to sing the praises of the world? Why is it that the soul in grief can feel an expansion of love which reaches to the stars? These are mysteries to me. I know only that sometime in the third year after my wife died, I felt myself more acutely aware that each of us is truly a living consciousness of death, and that each of us has a vocation to become a spokesperson for all that is fading but, at this moment, endures. The grief that followed the death of my wife eventually softened the hard shell of my mind and splintered its habits and routines. Grief was the awful teacher who immersed me in the ancient rhythms of the soul, rhythms which seem to follow the wheel of the stars.

At times now I have the strange impression that I am breathing in harmony with the things of the world, that between me and the world there is a conspiracy, a rhythmic exchange of our breaths. In one of his letters, Rilke remarks on this strange intercourse between us and the world. Our task, he felt, was to attend to the provisional and perishable character of the earth and its things so passionately and with a fullness of love, that their essential being would arise again invisibly in us. In this context, he called us "bees of the invisible,"[4] which seems to me to be a fine and evocative image for this work of transforming lament over loss into praise and song. Grief had brought me so far from the world that I had known and taken for granted, that I found myself so many times in a state of bewildered amazement at the newness of the world. Lingering near things in such moments, I have felt like the bee who transforms the nectar of the flower, its liquid juice, into sweet honey. Breathing in the aroma of bird and tree, wind and river, stone and star, I have felt at times, and still do, as if I am harvesting the honey of their scented breath. In these moments, the fixed meanings which the world and its things have for me dissolve, and something of their soul and mine come together. In these moments of con-spiracy, words seem to drip with the blue honey of the world.

Earlier I noted how mourning is a greening process, how grief and the long, slow winter season of mourning plunge us into the green ripeness of the soul and its vegetative rhythms. The lyrical improvisations of this chapter and the two which follow are green leafy songs sung in praise of the world, soul songs sung in its journey through grief and after the long slow winter of mourning have been endured. As Rilke says,

> More knowing would he bend the willows' branches who has experienced the willows' roots.[5]

THE VOICES OF THE WORLD ~

THE SPIDER'S WEB

> *The web, about one foot in diameter and perhaps even larger, was framed in the bright light of a full, yellow moon. Stretched across a narrow path in the driveway, it hung suspended between the low branch of a tree and the corner of the house. A slight breeze made it vibrate, and for a moment it seemed as if I could hear a sound when the wind played the spider's creation as a musical instrument. What struck me most was the size of the web and the way in which its filaments hung like threads of silver, the color and shape of a snowflake, or like a cold*

blue-silver star in the far distance of space. Its delicacy was elegant, wispy threads whose seeming fragility was in fact the secret of its strength. Yielding to the wind, the web was an architectural marvel certainly revealing the genius of its maker.

The architect, a spider, was there in the web, and in the brilliance of the moon's light I could see its dance of creation. Spinning the web out of itself, creating a landscape from its own movements, the spider was making a world out of its own body. For a long time I stood there, watching this scene of creation, feeling as if I were witnessing the birth of a universe. As I watched, I wondered what the creator of that world, the spider, knew of me. If I touched the web, carefully rocking it with one finger, I would enter into its world as a vibration. Reimagined in this way as a vibrational presence in the spider's world, I realized that I am, that we are, always plural, always more than what we know and think of ourselves, a galaxy of possibilities as vast and numberless as the stars in a clear midnight sky.

Spider's webs and our webs of meaning! We are spinners too, spinners of tall tales and sad stories, of midnight visions and cosmic dreams. In its web, its own world, the spider seems at home. When my wife died, I realized that I was not so comfortably at home in the worlds of meaning we had made for each other. Her death shattered the foundations of my world, and I saw how quickly the breath of death can blow apart the flimsy shelters of security we build for ourselves against the anxiety of losing what we love and what we have. In his *Duino Elegies,* Rilke makes the same point:

and already the knowing brutes are aware

that we don't feel very securely at home
within our interpreted world.[6]

How much I envied this spider at this moment. A kind of
enchantment overtook me, and for a while I became its prey. Not, of
course, to be eaten, but to be transformed, emptied out of myself and
invited to dream. And in this moment of reverie, when the passage of
time was suspended, when the counting of minutes no longer mattered,
I passed through the web and for a moment felt enlarged in my being.
Web as star and stars as webs spun by invisible beings! "In reverie,"
Bachelard notes, "we re-enter into contact with possibilities which
destiny has not been able to make use of."[7]

In this remarkably unimportant encounter with the spider in its
web, I sensed the secret harmonies of the universe, and I felt the
invisible connections among all elements of creation, the affinity of
each thing for every other thing. A moment of reverie around a spider's
web was one of those brief moments when I did feel that death was in
support of life, that death was, in fact, opening me to a feeling of joy
for the simple, even the simplest, occasions of life. My earlier envy at
its utter simplicity was now transformed into a prayer of gratitude. On
a moonlit night, and in complete surprise, this small being gave me a
little joy. It was a small step in homecoming, taken near the end of the
second year after she had gone.

In moments like this one, I have felt addressed by the things of
the world, called by them. And always, it seems, it is the simple things
which call, those things that linger near the margins of our day-to-day
living and often go unnoticed. Simple, and yet at times, awesome too,
like angels who also wait near the edges of the world. Is it not curious
to discover that things so seemingly different, like angels and spiders,
share a secret? When grief released me back into life, I discovered that
the spider is as much a miracle as is the angel, that it, as much as the
angel, has the power to release the numinous in the ordinary, the

sacred contained within the profane. A spider's web, the sound of church bells on an early Sunday morning, a shaft of light on the stones of an ancient, empty church: each of these things holds a secret seed of the sacred and has this power to free us into simple joy.

Walt Whitman in, "A Noiseless Patient Spider," captures these qualities:

A noiseless patient spider,
I mark'd whereon a little promontory it stood isolated,
Mark'd how to explore the vacant vast surrounding,
It launch'd forth filament, filament, filament out of itself,
Ever unreeling down, ever tirelessly speeding them.

And you o my soul where you stand,
Surrounded, detached, in measureless oceans of space,
Ceaselessly musing, venturing, throwing, seeking the spheres to connect them,
Till the bridge you will need be form'd, till the ductile
                    anchor hold,
Till the gossamer thread you fling catch somewhere, o
my soul.[8]

Through these lines the poet connects the spider's work and the work of our souls. We, like the noiseless, patient spider launch filaments out of ourselves, threads of hope and dream, until the bridge we need with the world and with others is formed. The gossamer threads of meaning we fling catch hold somewhere and, for a moment, secure us a place.

"Poets," Bachelard wrote, "speak the language of the world."[9] So too do we when grief frees us to rejoice again in life, when it lets go of us and enlarges our heart and its capacity to love again. In these moments, I have felt that the depths of my soul were being stirred into wakefulness by the appeal of things. And, in such moments, I have wondered where the boundaries of my soul and the soul of things are drawn, because so often it has felt as if there was a fabric being woven between them. So, I wonder if Whitman's poem is only one more filament of the spider launched forth out of itself in exploration of the vacant, vast, measureless oceans of space. Is the poet's poem as much the spider's work, its way of further realizing itself, as the poem is the work of the poet? Is the poem the spider's way of realizing and speaking itself? Is the spider speaking of Whitman, as much as Whitman is speaking of the spider?

After the initial shocks of grief and the long winter of mourning, after feeling released into life and quiet joy again, I cannot help but imagine that it is the web which spins the poem as much as it is the poem which speaks the web, and that the poem is as much the spider speaking of the poet as it is the poet musing on the spider. This curious reversal of our ordinary way of understanding our place in creation, when we imagine ourselves somehow outside and in charge of it, is an unexpected gift of grief endured and transformed into a newfound sense of joy in living.

THE BIRD'S SONG

> Faith is the bird that feels the light
> And sings when the dawn is still dark.[10]

> Hope is the thing with feathers
> That perches in the soul.[11]

It was not yet light, the moment just before the day, the last moment of the night. The hills were still dark, but their jagged edges were already ribboned and outlined with a soft hue, crowning them in purple. It was a knife-edge moment when the world was still deciding whether it would slip back into sleep, or stretch itself to become another dawn. One of those rare moments when you actually do sense that the sunrise is never a guarantee, when it seems that each dawn is a decision made again and again by the world itself. If you are awake in such a moment before the dawn, that last second before the choice is made, you know that everything which you continuously anticipate, the entire round world of all creation, could fold back into eternal night. And you stand, then, poised on that knife edge, motionless within the moment, wrapped in its stillness, waiting for the world to renew itself again. In such moments you are empty; you are only an empty waiting.

At first I hardly noticed—the sound was so soft, and it seemed so singular, so far away. But it was enough for those few notes of the bird to awaken me. I stirred, and the song began to build. The solitary singer became a chorus, and over there by the hills the light exploded in a joyful song of delight. Song and light had begun, and in this first moment of the new day it seemed as if the entire space of the world would not be large enough to hold this swelling song of the spreading light.

When God made the world, birds sang. This is a secret which the morning song of the bird teaches me each dawn, every morning: light is song, song is light! When the dawn comes, the bird begins to sing, and song is brought into the world. When the bird begins to sing, dawn comes, and light is brought into the world. Song and light are one and the same.

But to be able to hear this great secret of creation—that light sings the world into being and song lightens the world—requires a radical shift in our ways of understanding the world and living in it. For me, this shift was the earthquake of the soul which happened with the death of my wife. In the aftershocks of grief, and especially in the frozen winter of mourning, I lost touch with anything that was meaningful or useful. What did it matter to me now that I had a house, that I paid my bills on time, that I was a good citizen who had lived by the rules and obeyed the law? I cared nothing for any of that, and in this condition I was being made ready for a change.

The change came when, sometime in the beginning of the third year after my wife's death, mourning yielded to melancholy, when small, shoots of green joy began to puncture the dead and barren landscape of my winter soul. In the sweet happiness of melancholy, in that gentle state of feeling newly born, I discovered a kind of presence which precedes meaning and makes all our meaning-making possible. The dawn song of the bird, a most useless thing, evoked a presence which understands that, when the dawn comes and the bird sings, the song is a celebration of the light. That is all! The early morning light is the song of the bird, and the bird's early morning song is the light of creation. A beautiful kinship renewed each morning, a continual reminder of the love between the morning light and the song of the bird, a love song. All of this is really nothing, nothing at all. But all of it is really everything.

So many mornings now I feel called to participate in this nothing, this full emptiness of the world which is everything. In these moments of dawn, I awake more slowly without hurry to plan the day or to make sense of it. The bird sings its song, light softly creeps into the world, and I am free of the burdens of being anything but this moment. To gather some new bits of information about the weather or the stock market or the political state of the nation would be in such a moment a betrayal of the gifts which the world is always offering us, gifts which are like morning fruit to nourish the soul. I know nothing when I am sung into wakefulness by the light-song of the bird. I am only, at best, a witness to this exuberant epiphany of the world, and that is all that I am asked to be. But, surrendering to this invitation, I am renewed, and the world's dawn is matched by a dawn in my soul. I wish to sing in this moment, and in my song acknowledge my gratitude for being rescued from the lonely isolation of my own mind, for being webbed into this larger fabric of creation. Hope, and joy, truly are singing birds which perch in the soul. We need only to lend an ear.

THE BALLET OF THE WHALE

I was walking with a friend on the beach, engaged in meaningful conversation about a patient. Trading fantasies disguised as theory, we went back and forth in a dialogue about dynamics and diagnoses, about treatment strategies and the burdens of psychotherapy. Embraced by the world but rather oblivious to it, we took for granted how receptive the landscapes of the world are to human words. Passing rock and shell, bird and wave, we never gave a thought to their impressions of our conversation. Our world of words had closed in on itself. Our world had become rounded like a bubble in which we floated over and slightly above the sand and the shells, momentarily cut off from the breeze and the sound of the waves.

Who saw it first is difficult to say—the experience began as something less than a vision, and something more of a feeling. When the whale's spray spouted above the surface of the water, the bubble of meaning in which we were encased—almost entombed—was broken, and it was that shift in the landscape which registered the whale's presence. Like air rushing out of a closed chamber, the whale drew from each of us only the sound of air escaping from our bodies. Silenced by the depth of the moment, we stood still, gasping for a word, gazing in awe. "Look!" That was all we could say, a word accompanied by a raised hand and a finger pointing toward the water.

"Look!" A command that felt as if it were spoken to us rather than by us. "Look!" A single word and a simple gesture that felt as if it were the whale's own command spoken through us.

Such moments which would silence our meaning-making in the world can only be obeyed, and in reply to our obedience the whale began its ballet. Over and over again it dove and then breached the surface, its fluke delicately poised in the air, like a dancer at the apogee of her jump, before breaking the surface of the water. Its dance had deepened our space, refigured it as a place of joy, and drew each of us out of the interior depths of our psychological spaces into the aesthetic depths of the world. Every angel, because of its beauty, is terrible, Rilke says. So too is the whale, a terrible, awe-ful beauty whose epiphanies explode the narrow chambers of the human mind.

The whale danced and danced again, and before it departed its ballet had spread beyond itself to envelop not only our bodies, but also those of a school of dolphins swimming nearby. The dolphins joined the dance, and in graceful, sweeping arcs they choreographed an accompaniment to the whale's presence. The ballet of the whale had radiated across the landscape, whale becoming dolphin, dolphin becoming ocean, ocean becoming earth, earth becoming sky, sky becoming us, each and all of us becoming an echo of the other, deepening and refiguring the presence of all. In the splendor of this moment, myriad forms of life resonated with each other. We were emptied of ourselves, delivered of who we were, and received by the round dance of creation. For a moment it felt as if we had found our way home. And for that moment it was enough.

The ballet of a whale, like the spider spinning its web and the bird singing its morning song, is a moment of beauty in the world. Each of these moments are invitations to explore and experience the world's aesthetic depths. Now, when I can allow myself to be embraced by these occasions, when I can let myself sink in reverie below the busyness of my mind, when I can honor how the death of my wife opened my soul, I am also honoring her in sadness and in joy. In these moments, I marvel at the power of grief to open the soul to the hidden and forgotten radiance of beauty in the world. Why should grief and beauty be companions in the soul, I do not know, nor would I have ever dreamed of their relation in those early times of grief, and less in the long winter of mourning. But they are, or at least this is how it has been for me. I can only add that these eruptions of beauty empty me in so complete a way that I have no name and no history. Gaston Bachelard speaks of reverie in this way. He says that in states of reverie we are liberated from the narrow confines of our psychological identities and awakened to our place within the weave of creation. Whether it be bird, spider, or whale, or whether it be the slant of fading afternoon light on a rain-washed street or the sound of church bells on an early Sunday morning, these small, useless miracles open the world's treasures and establish us as cosmic citizens. On the other side of grief, it is possible to dream cosmic dreams.

Learning to dream with the world in this way, learning to muse in reverie around simple things, has helped to mend the fissures in my broken soul. Perhaps, too, it also helps in some small way to increase the well-being of earth and even the stars. But I make no claim here about this possibility. I do not even hold onto it as a hope. I know only this: the soul fractured in grief can be healed by the world's charm, and that this healing is not really about doing anything, but about a way of being. I want less from the world now, much less than ever before. In my best moments now, in those moments when my soul can sing its lyrical improvisations in celebration of the world, I have only a kind of care-ful regard for the world. On these occasions of re-gard, I take a second look, with softer eyes. My soul is a-mused by the world, called and awakened by the muse of things, by that sacred seed which the ordinary harbors in its beauty.

CHAPTER

6

In the Early Morning of the World

READING AND DREAMING ~

The room was silent except for the rhythmic ticking of a grandfather clock in the hallway. It was cold, the chill in the house not yet warmed by the feeble early morning light. But I was accustomed to these moments before the day began, moments when I took simple pleasure in wrapping myself in a bathrobe and blanket to sit still and motionless in my rocking chair. Since the death of my wife eighteen months earlier, the bed always seemed a cold and empty place, and, waking early in the morning, I always sought refuge in this quiet oasis of solitude.

I loved these moments and the setting, and I especially loved the melancholic mood which marked these occasions. I felt a kind of sad peace in this melancholy, a feeling which seemed to be composed of two equal parts. On one hand, I always felt as if, from the vantage point of my rocking chair, I was seeing things for the last time, as if I could sense in the very presence of things their fading. On the other hand, in the early morning light, I also felt as if I was seeing things for the first time, as if I was witnessing not only the start of the day but also the true origins of the world.

Such a feeling was reminiscent of an earlier time in my life, when, as a young boy, I would venture outside my home in the early morning in order to be present to the day as it was beginning. These were the halcyon days of summer when school was finished and I felt liberated into another, different identity, when, in fact, I was no longer the child of my parents but a stranger in this beautiful world. Often, I would simply sit on a bench, and, while watching a colony of ants or the floating arcs of a butterfly, I would daydream. In these moments, I knew that I had come from elsewhere and that these occasions were times for recollecting that other place beyond this time and space. When, finally, the day would begin, when the grown-ups would enter the day on their way to work, I was always somewhat disappointed at the loss of this moment, when the world had a newness about it, a fresh quality which gave me a quiet sense of joy. I also felt sad at being robbed of a secret about the origins of things, sad about this loss of contact with origins.

I believe, now, that the loss of my wife opened up for me not only a sorrow about my own personal origins, about our past together which now no longer had a future, but also reopened those earlier moments of an origin beyond a personal history. I believe now that melancholy is a kind of crucible where loss and origins blend together, where grief and its cloudy, liquid sorrows, momentarily clear, and we get a glimpse of our true home and catch a brief vision of the face we had before we were born. The lyrical improvisations sung in celebration of the world in this chapter have this undertone of a return to origins as a path back into life.

As I look back now, I know that in those moments it was not I who was sitting in that rocking chair patiently waiting in the stillness and silence for the return of that something I once had but had left behind. No! In those early morning moments, when the light was still so soft and vulnerable that it broke the hardness of my heart, it was the Orphan, that melancholic companion of the soul in grief, who sat still and motionless in that chair.

On some of these mornings, the waiting was accompanied by the reading of a book. To be more precise, I was not exactly reading a book; the book was more like an occasion for slipping into a state of reverie, in which my conscious mind fell into the dreaming state of the soul. "We were reading and now we are dreaming,"[1] Gaston Bachelard says of reverie, and I can attest to this power of reverie to dissolve the boundaries between us and the world. In this between place, I would find myself a part of what I was experiencing rather than apart from it, safely ensconced in the small chambers of my own ego-mind. In this happy place, I inhabited the world in such a way that the taken-for-granted parameters of space and time temporarily disappeared. I was never surprised, therefore, that through the book as an occasion for reverie, an entire morning could slip by. How pleasant it was to while away a whole morning in the solitude of reverie, to discover that dawn had brightened into a sun yellow afternoon.

Melancholy has this same power to loosen the soul from the shackles of the mind and to plunge us into that place where we feel ourselves solicited by the world, especially by the appeal which the perishable things of the world make, even in the moment of their highest flowering. Within melancholy's grasp, we sense that "Life becomes immense when we start recognizing that there is no assurance that we will live out this day."[2] No assurance either that those whom we most love will walk through the door again at the end of the day. One moment my wife was there in the room with me, and then she was gone. This recognition of the fragile and temporary presence of those whom we love, this recognition more than anything else, now shapes my way of living.

I admit that this is a difficult place to be, this place where you feel like you are a witness to the blooming and the fading of the world. It is a sad place, and yet a place too that is scented with a kind of peace and joy. In my life now I insist on the right to my melancholy. It is the small treasure that lies buried under the frozen fields of mourning. Anyone who has endured that winter landscape, anyone who by some miracle has survived the bone breaking blasts of the winter winds of the soul, deserves to celebrate the thaw which uncovers this treasure.

I cannot accept, therefore, the idea that melancholy is a neurotic condition. But this is precisely the view which Sigmund Freud espoused in his seminal essay "Mourning and Melancholia."[3] For Freud, melancholia was a failed mourning, specifically a kind of denial on the part of the ego-mind to let go of the one who has died. In place of a gradual process of letting go of the other who has died (or to use the more correct if formidable language of psychoanalysis, a gradual detachment of the ego's libido from the lost object), which characterizes the condition of mourning, the melancholic individual unconsciously identifies with the lost other. He or she then continues to behave as if the other has not died and in doing so continuously repeats the past, looking to find in others a duplicate of what has been lost. In a sense the melancholic one is entombed in a dead past.

My experience of melancholy, however, convinces me that it is precisely the opposite of what Freud said. Melancholy did not chain me to the past. On the contrary, it liberated me into the present, where I am more attentive to the tenuous beauty of the moment, more appreciative of it. In melancholy, I linger just a little longer with the other, perhaps to take a deeper look or perhaps to hold the hand just a fraction longer, because I know now that this moment will never come again.

I believe Freud missed this poignant character of melancholy because he was looking at grief and mourning from the vantage point of the ego-mind and not, strangely enough, from the vantage point of the soul. I know for myself that there were many moments when I felt hustled and hurried back into busyness, and I was even somewhat criticized for my melancholy. To some of my friends, it was as if I was wallowing in a slough of despair. But I was not. On the contrary, I was being led by the soul on its winter journey through mourning, living according to its rhythms which were beyond my control. In mourning, the soul was dissolving my own personal loss in the larger story of love and loss which characterizes the round of all creation.

The journey of grief through mourning into melancholy always has this power to connect us to this larger story of love and loss, a story which reaches even to the stars. I know that there have been many moments when the vast expanse of the night sky has been the exact mirror of my melancholic soul, when this midnight sky embraced me, made me feel at home, and filled me with a sense that what I once had and had lost or forgotten or left behind was this cosmic connection, this feeling that I did belong to the round dance of a divine, holy creation. In this respect, the patients whom Freud saw were, I believe, expressing through their personal sorrows the hunger of the ego-mind for this connection, a connection which was lost when centuries ago we severed our ties to the world and created that ego-mind which with its symptoms limped into Freud's consulting room in the latter part of the last century.[4] Through personal loss and the mourning process, the modern ego-mind was expressing its grief over its lost relation to the soul and its wider field of love. In this respect, I believe that melancholy is a way the soul deepens mind and seeks to restore to personal life, its collective and transpersonal dimensions.

It was this larger story of loss and grief speaking through the mourning, but Freud lacked the cosmic vision to hear it. To hear the melancholy of the soul as something other than a neurotic symptom, we would, in fact, have to go back to an earlier time, perhaps five hundred years ago, when melancholia, the older term which Freud in fact used, was one of four styles of temperament. In addition to the melancholic, there was the sanguine one, the phlegmatic one, and the choleric one. Each of them described a person whose basic mood or disposition was the expression of a complex relation between the humours of the body and the stars. If we have lost our appreciation for these terms, it is because we have lost our connection to the larger picture where soul and star are one.

My own grief, mourning, and the melancholy which has flowered from them, have led me back to this appreciation of the larger story. The soul's way has been the guide, and on its path I have come to cherish the singularity of each moment, each one of which will never come again, and any one of which could be the last.

WIND

The room was quiet and illumined only by the light of a candle. Its warmth contrasted sharply with the cold November night beyond its walls. The sound of wind chimes softened the edges and infused the room with a feeling of some faraway place. Their melody carried the song of the wind, and each note appealed to my heart to remember something once known but now forgotten. I relaxed into the wind's song. My breathing no longer seemed to come only from within but was now all around me, as if the room and the cold November night breathed in harmony. I was myself and yet not myself, something other, something suddenly more. The familiar distinction of I/not I no longer made sense. The song of the wind and the sound of my breathing were one and the same.

LIGHT

The light seemed young, like the first dawn. It had a soft feel on the skin, like morning mist, and a diaphanous, veil-like quality which filtered the light and gave it a pale yellow hue. This dreamy early morning glow spread itself over a smooth landscape undisturbed in its features, save for a few low hills in the distance. There were no sounds. A stillness so perfect, so pure, complete within itself: full, tranquil, a moment without any horizons of memory or desire.

Enveloped in the mist, wrapped within this light, I was not separate from it. It was as if I was the consciousness of that light itself, the way in which light is conscious, the way in which we might imagine consciousness first entered the world. This light seemed an older, more archaic sense of "I", perhaps the very thing which the song of the wind was promising when it beckoned me to remember something long forgotten. I was dispersed as light, no longer apart from the landscape. How long I dreamed in this way is impossible to say, but the moment suddenly changed with something like a quantum leap in the light's awareness of itself. There, bathed in the light, a being as radiant as the light itself appeared, a being beautiful in a form before all distinctions, a being possessed of itself, content, tranquil, undisturbed, simply there; a presence, perhaps even formed from the light itself, a condensation of the light, the light's own self-awareness. And lying next to it, as if kin, a being equally beautiful: black, sleek, muscular, toned with animal passion and energy, but equally in repose, still, unmoving, except for the occasional motion of its tail, a being also formed from the light.

The stillness continued. Nothing stirred except, on occasion, the tail of the animal, as if some pregnancy in this field of light was awaiting its moment of deliverance.

Enduring patience seemed mixed with ripening anticipation. And then a sound, the voice of the light itself, as if this consciousness had gathered itself to speak: "In the early morning of the world, when the Angel and the Panther were one . . ."

Kathleen Raine, a poet, scholar, and friend who has been a companion on these journeys, writes the following in her *Autobiographies*:

> I remember the palpable stillness of that pine plantation, the fir-cones lying where they fell on the carpet of needles muting sound in a place shunned by all life but that of the trees themselves, with their branches forever dying away below to form overhead an endlessly entangled dead thicket. In my fear of its dusk was also an exaltation in the experience of the wood-in-itself, as another vista of awareness into which consciousness could flow. The circumference of consciousness was the circumference of the perceptible world; the world perceived was that consciousness, that consciousness the world: there was no distinction between seer and seen, knowledge and its object.

She writes these words in memory of a childhood, in a chapter called "Farewell Happy Fields." Reflecting on that time she adds the following:

> Perhaps those called 'nature-mystics' simply retain longer than others our normal consciousness, our birthright, lost sooner or later, or returning only rarely; or it is we who return only rarely, and lose Eden by a turning away, a refusing to look. Our separate identity grows over us like a skin, or shroud.[5]

These reveries of light and wind, nursed in melancholy, take me beyond myself, home to that faraway place in the early mornings of the world. They take me to that place which Kathleen Raine describes as the Eden from which we have turned. These reveries are so deep that they rid me of my history, so deep that they liberate me from my name, a possibility of reverie which Gaston Bachelard notes in his meditations on this topic.[6]

Such moments when I have felt it possible to forget my history and, for a moment, even if only for a moment, even to let go of my name, have been true gifts in the midst of sorrow. They raise that thick curtain of isolation which grief had placed between me and the world. In these moments, I have trembled with an impossible and unexpected sense of joy at feeling connected at a cellular level with the resonant vibrations of all creation. French poet Jean Follain wrote:

> When there falls from the hands of the serving girl
> the pale round plate
> the color of the clouds
> the pieces must be picked up
> while the chandelier trembles
> in the master's dining room.[7]

One must be just a trifle mad to believe these lines, and only after the madness induced by loss have I been able to affirm their truth of a solidarity among all the beings of that house, among servant and master, plate and chandelier. As a child, perhaps, I knew of this mysterious resonance among things, but I have long ago said farewell to those happy fields. How can I possibly understand now that my wife's death has led me back to these places, has, in a sense, made me childlike again, at least in my best moments, when I no longer turn away? When I can release into these moments, I understand the animation of the world, and I am drawn into the secret life of things and touched by them. When I read these lines from a long forgotten poet, I cannot be indifferent to how things can tremble for each other, how they can be affected by the plight of their companions, moved by what might even be called a death of one of their kind. Melancholy dissolves that skin or shroud of identity which Kathleen Raine speaks of. Emptied of myself in these moments, I am extended deeper into the world, and it seems as if for a time I am returning from the turn I made so long ago.

THE WATER HOLE

I waited there early in the morning, just before the sun began to rise. It was cool and silent, and in the hide you are invisible, like an unseen witness to a drama: the arrival of the animals at the water hole. They came in groups, collections of their kind, appearing out of the mist of the bush almost miraculously. Where a moment ago there had been nothing but the dry African plain, animals now appeared as if born by the bush itself, creatures formed out of the morning mist. The bush was now the womb of time pouring life onto what had been an empty, silent landscape. The animals' appearance was effortless, slow, graceful, silent. The breath of God stirring over the formless waters of creation? It was dawn, and it could have been the very first day.

The silence was overwhelming. Not the absence of sound—one hears the animals, birds, and other sounds of the bush—rather a silence containing no human sound, a landscape echoing our exclusion, a silence speaking our absence. A sleepy kind of dumbness lay over this landscape of mist and bush and animal and sun and cool morning breeze and water. Earth was in repose, folded in on itself and asleep.

The land grew empty again. As silently as they had appeared out of the early morning, the animals disappeared back into the bush. They were taken back into invisibility, dissolved again into formless mist. If I waited long enough, could I also dissolve into that landscape, could I be received by the mist in the endless cycle of appearance and disappearance, of form and dissolution?

The silence of the land said 'No!' I had already been placed at a distance. (Or is it that I had placed myself at a distance?) The silence of the bush had spoken: the earth had been waking itself through our minds for countless ages. Earth itself had broken the cycle of repetition; through us it had been coming to its own realization. The poet Rilke had known this secret: 'Earth! Isn't this what you want: an invisible rearising within us?' [8] Into that silence there had come word. Into that silence had come language. Through the word we had become (or were we chosen to be?) agents of the earth.

Agents of the earth! Poets sow strange seeds, but perhaps they reap the most bountiful and truthful harvest. Perhaps technology has been part of the earth's long history of coming to know itself, and in that effort we have been its servant. The silence of that African plain, however, suggests how dispensable we really are. It echoes an absence and perhaps even our eventual disappearance. On a dry African plain, in the silence of the early morning, I began to imagine technology as a vocation, as the earth's call to us to become its agent and instrument of awakening. But, then, in a moment of sorrow, my imagination faltered and I felt small and too insignificant for such a task. I felt too far away from the animals and the earth, too far away from home. Perhaps all our glorious technological achievements were not the earth's way of coming to know itself but more the earth's way of coming to cleanse itself of us. [9]

Melancholy has a bittersweet taste to it, and there are these occasions when I do feel how far I have come from being in repose with the world. Loss has attuned me to larger separations, and there are times when I know how much I have distanced myself from the rest of creation and have forgotten the claim that the order of life makes upon me. But star and stone, angel and panther, wind and tree continue in their appeals. In a strange way which I could never have predicted, the sweetness of melancholy has opened me to these appeals.

Even today, seven years after Janet's death, there are moments when events and experiences which preceded her death make their forceful emotional claim to become part of my living present. On these occasions I fall into the soul's temporal rhythms, and, in ways which my reason cannot fathom, I am not remembering an event which happened before Janet died. Rather, I am living that event in the moment. I am living it as if for the first time. These experiences fracture our ordinary boundaries of space and time. Within this vortex of time, my personal loss is generally placed within a larger field; it takes on an archetypal dimension. The following tale of the leopard has been one of these occasions.

IF THE LEOPARD COMES

It was already late in the evening when we gathered to wait and watch for the leopard's return. Earlier in the day we had found the fresh remains of a partially eaten bush buck. For some reason, the leopard had not protected it from scavengers, and we had spent the morning doing its work. Lifting the buck into a tree, its blood dripped onto our hands and clothing, binding us and the leopard together.

Framed by the branches and leaves of the tree where we had placed the buck, the moon was larger and closer to the earth than I had ever seen it. Its yellow surface spread a cold white light onto the landscape, while to the right of us and beyond the tree, the bush reached deeply into a soft, inviting blackness. We waited without speaking. Watched by the moon we remained in the night silence for the leopard to return.

I slipped into a reverie, or was it a dream? When night came, our early ancestors would have gathered in the darkness, drawn together by their fear. The leopard would have been out there, and the ancestors would be waiting for morning. For a few, however, the moon and its pale white light would draw away the fear, and these few would wonder about the moon and what it was. Dimly, on the edge of a consciousness not yet fully born, they would feel drawn beyond the bush. The moon would overcome the leopard.

Immersed in this reverie—was it a dream? I heard what Neil Armstrong said when he first landed on the moon in 1969: "Hello Houston. Tranquillity base here. The Eagle has landed!"

I awoke with a start. The night had grown colder. Michael, our guide, seemed to be asleep. Our tracker, Joe, still atop the hood of our vehicle, was motionless. The bush was silent except for the sounds of an occasional bird. The moon which earlier was so near was now far away and small. I felt cold, and I wondered how far we had come waiting for the leopard.

We waited, but the leopard never came. We were too far away, strangers watched now by the leopard with a

*dim remembrance of kinship. The moon had separated
us and was now a measure of our distance.*

    *When the sun began to rise we drove away. The
leopard had won. It had waited, and I knew then that it
would continue to wait for our return. We had left the
bush so long ago, but the leopard was still with us, and
this, I felt, it knew. Throughout the long night it had been
waiting for us, but we were not yet ready. It would
continue to wait.* [10]

Before Janet died, I had a vague sense that life was really a straight
line, and I lived my life half committed to this unexamined prescription.
I was responsible, and only on occasion did I explore a wilder, less
conventional life. But these explorations were mostly the dreams of a
reluctant gypsy soul, and for the most part I took very few risks.

After her death, however, my life coiled in on itself, and since then
I have come to appreciate how my life is much more circular in its
movements. Perhaps I always knew it but forgot. I remember that two
years before she died, I had a vivid glimpse of the way in which a simple
event, like sitting on a park bench on a lazy Sunday afternoon, was the
occasion for revealing how a singular moment in time can turn round
on itself and open to archaic depths.

> A man sits on a park bench
> dreaming his life away.
> "Have I been here before?" he wonders.
> His father, now long dead, appears.
> Did he too sit on this bench,
> dreaming his life away?
>
> Who is the father, who is the son?
>
> In the middle way, the turning comes,
> and the shape of life becomes a circle.

Then, for the first time,
you see the ending of your life
through the beginning.
At that moment he knew
that the soul has always been ahead of him,
waiting for him at this place,
waiting for him to turn and close the circle,
waiting for him to gather all the roads he has traveled
and come back home.[11]

From the Panther in the early morning of the world to the leopard waiting in the bush, my life seems always to have been spiraling around the same themes of departure, love, loss, and the journey home. And, I believe now that my soul has always known all this. The sad fact, however, is that I had to be reminded of the soul's wisdom through the loss of the woman I loved. I do not mean to suggest, or even imply, that I think of my wife's death as a sacrifice made on behalf of my education. I mean to say only that her death was an earthquake of my soul which has forced me to change my life in the direction of these deeper currents of the soul. If I could not always be as faithful and true to her in life as I wanted to be, I now owe her, and myself, that fidelity to whom she was, and is, as well as to whom I am, and, I believe, whom she knew me to be.

The line of time has been broken by death. Now, each moment can be like a magnet which draws to itself all those related moments of a life, not so much, however, as a repetition, but more as a deepening which colors this time with older ones. Grief and its aftershocks force me to look at the world through the soul's non-linear, vertical time, where the personal moment is washed in deeper, ancient waters. In these moments, I always have the sense that something of me has been here before and that I am coming home.

ANCIENT WHISPERS

I came back to that place in Africa where ten years earlier the leopard had waited. Much in my life had happened since that encounter, but the leopard, it seems, was always there, prowling the margins of consciousness, a shadow in the half-light of reverie and dream, a faint sound always in the distance. Grief had brought me to the edges of the world, and now some three years after my wife's death I had returned with the woman from the wild hills of Devon, England whom one day I would marry.

We were staying in one of the protected game reserves and decided to return to the water hole. We would spend the night in a tree house situated about three miles from the base camp. It was quite open and seemed almost unprotected as we prepared our vigil.

The night was chilly and the sky clear. Stars were abundant, pale blue flecks of light arranged in patterns unfamiliar to us. We lay there together, listening for the sound of animals, our eyes drawn toward the heavens. Sleep came, bringing with it African dreams.

It was not a nocturnal dream that startled me that night. It was something else, something closer to a waking dream, a visitation, a reverie. Exactly what it was that awakened me I do not know. There, in the tree house, off to the side, was a leopard. It just appeared as if formed out of the night air, like the panther in the early morning of the world seemed to arise from the light. The leopard remained still, watching me with its pale yellow eyes. There was no movement, and strangely, I felt not fear but wonder.

The leopard gave a low, rumbling growl, a deep throaty sound which seemed to come from both the animal before me and some distant place and time. There were no words but I heard a language in that sound. A growl like the whisper of an ancient, common tongue, calling me back to a communion we once shared, so long ago, perhaps as long ago as the early morning of the world. The leopard growled once more and disappeared. It did not walk away. It just disappeared, as if the air from which it had congealed had now dispersed.

Honestly, I do not know what to make of such a moment, but I tell it because it does belong to the journey which grief initiated in my soul. So many moments of that journey have been spent in a state of melancholic reverie that reverie is, perhaps, the most apt term for the experience. In these experiences, I have felt myself to be so fully present in and to the moment that the usual distinction between myself and the occasion has melted away. During these times, I have been in a between place, neither perceiving the world with open eyes, nor dreaming a world with eyes fully closed. Melancholic reverie escorts me beyond these dichotomies, and in its grasp I view the world with a softer eye, often obliquely.

In the corners of experience, and on its often neglected margins, the world reveals its imaginal depths to the soul. These epiphanies are awe-ful, that is, filled with awe. They are moments of mystery when the familiar boundary of mind and world is reversed or even erased. The painter Paul Klee knew this moment of reversal. "In a forest," he said, "I have felt many times over that it was not I who looked at the forest. Some days I felt that the trees were looking at me, were speaking to me."[12]

In addition, these moments are also occasions when the usual sequence of past, present, and future collapses to disclose in each moment the lingering presence of a time before time which is nevertheless now. Sometimes, I wonder if these occasions of reversal and collapse are what were once more commonly and easily called miracles. Maybe what our minds cannot accept, our souls readily experience, and maybe love and loss prepare us again for such miracles.

But, again, I do not know, and I make no claim for these experiences beyond saying that they did happen. Grief, the long, slow winter of mourning, and the melancholic reverie which has followed have made me a happy stranger in this world. I love the dawn in ways I would have never thought possible before, and the rain, and the song of birds, and the whole rich panoply of daily wonders and miracles. And in this place, I find that I must accept what Gaston Bachelard says of the powers of reverie to change us. "In studying [only] the real man, the psychology of observation," Bachelard writes, "only encounters an uncrowned being."[13] Grief and mourning dissolve the strictures of conventional reality and prepare the way for melancholic reverie to restore the crown in a coronation of the soul. In this respect, love and loss can bring out the grace and dignity of the soul. As painful as the death of a loved one is, because we are flesh and flesh desires flesh, death can increase the boundary of love.

CHAPTER

7

Under the Starry Night Sky

LOVE AND DEATH~

> Someone blew the candle out,
> and now it is time to contemplate the stars.
> ~ *Veronica Goodchild, personal communication*

The candle! The light that we light, and the stars, the light that shines upon us, beckons us, and of which we are not the makers! When my wife died the candle that she and I had lit was extinguished, and her light vanished from this world. But now, under the starry night sky, there are moments when I can see her radiance shining brightly, and I know that she has become a brilliant star. Although the bonds of flesh hold very tightly after loss, I am convinced in these moments that love is stronger than death and that the stars of the heavenly night sky are formed from our gestures of love.

Dare we imagine that our gestures of love set up vibratory fields which can become stars, that the cosmos is the destiny of a soul that has learned how to love, and that this work of learning to love is why we are here? In a letter to Witold von Hulewicz, one of the Polish translators of his *Duino Elegies*, Rilke alludes to the work of love in this fashion: "Since the various materials in the cosmos are only the results of different rates of vibration, we are preparing in this way, not only intensities of a spiritual kind, but—who knows?—new substances, metals, nebulae and stars."[1] The work of love enlarges us, so much so that, as the Jungian analyst Maria-Louise von Franz notes, our gestures of love are the way in which we participate in the divine act of creation. For von Franz love is "such a fateful factor in the life of every human being because, more than anything else, it has the power to release the living from their ego-bound consciousness."[2]

On the headstone of my wife's grave, I had these words inscribed: "She opened my heart to love." Little did I realize when I chose those words how wide that opening would be. The work of loving is difficult, and yet, again as Rilke says, it is "the work for which all other work is but preparation." "Loving," he goes on to say, "is solitude, intensified and deepened loneness for him who loves," but it is also "high inducement to the individual to ripen." Love has blossomed from my sorrow, and in continuing this work of loving after loss, something in me has been ripened. But I would be untrue to the experience of my loss and the love which has followed, if I were to leave the impression that this ripening of my soul has had anything to do with my will. On the contrary, like the sun calls the flower, love is "something that chooses [the lover] out and calls him to vast things."[3] Love is a vocation which has opened my heart to the wide, infinite horizons of the stars. Sometimes, therefore, under the starry night sky, I have the feeling that the work of love is what allows the self to ripen as a star.

THE WINDOW AND THE WIND

Veronica and I were staying in a small village in the Tuscan hills of Italy. I was trying to put the finishing touches on an earlier version of this book. The house was an old converted water-mill. The room in which I was working overlooked a garden. I loved this room, especially at night, because the sky was often so brilliant with the cold light of the stars. I would light a candle, sit at my desk, and dream away several hours. But always the window overlooking the garden remained closed.

In an earlier book, I had written about how the closed window was the means by which we had been transformed into spectators of the world, detached from it and unmoved by it. [4] The book had brought me some measure of recognition, but in many ways I was unchanged by it. Something in me was still too much a spectator. And now, here I was nearly five years after the death of my wife, struggling to find words for a tragedy which did not allow for this safe distance and separation. In moments of melancholic reverie, my soul seemed to be hungering for a lost intimacy with the world. Indeed, there were moments when I could feel how I was part of the sap that strengthens the rose, how the blood which was pulsing through my veins reverberated with the thick, heavy juices that throbbed through stem and leaf and turned the flower toward the sun, how under a starry night sky I was suckled by the stars. But, sitting there by candlelight, the window remained closed.

One evening, however, a strong gust of wind forced the window open, and the light of the candle was extinguished. There was nothing extraordinary in this occurrence, except this: when the candle light disappeared, the room was flooded with stars. I felt as if I was sitting in a field of stars, that the distance between me and the stars had been eclipsed. Somehow, in this moment the separation between me and the world was dissolved, and for a moment I felt how true the kinship is between soul and star.

Someone blew the candle out, and it was time to contemplate the stars. I do not know what to make of this experience. Its meaning is ambiguous. Perhaps it means nothing at all; perhaps it was, after all, only a coincidence into which I am trying to read too much. While all this might be true, what remains, however, is the feeling tone of the experience. When the stars entered the darkened room, when they broke through the window of separation, I felt a deep sense of joy and an even deeper sense of love. Grief had isolated me from the world, and there I was trying to maintain this shield of protection, while at the same time the wilder currents of the soul were making me something more than a spectator to my wife's death. Grief was a breakdown of all that I was or ever imagined myself to be, and mourning was especially a slow, but continuous, erosion of my sense of self and its boundaries. Was this occasion a breakthrough of another way of being in the world, a way which softens those fixed boundaries between inside and outside, between soul and world?

Carl Jung describes such occasions as moments of synchronicity.[5] When a powerful state of psychological energy is constellated, the ordinary separation between soul and nature can collapse, so that events which occur in the world correspond in an acausal way with experiences which are taking place in the soul. Grief can be such an occasion. It can induce those powerful moments of soul, archetypal fields of energy, which have a transpersonal, collective character. For me, such moments were the occasion when my grief wore the mantle of the Orphan or the Angel, the occasion when my sense of loss was inscribed within a larger, more than personal, story. Perhaps the window and the wind was such an occasion, a moment of synchronicity, when the stars shattered the remaining remnants of a shipwrecked mind and touched the soul. But I make no claim here; I am only trying to follow the track of the experience wherever it leads me. It is, however, a curious, but significant, fact that according to von Franz Jung believed that "synchronistic events were always known only they were called in past times, signs of the gods or in Christian times miracles."[6] Maybe grief does have the power to break the mind and its will so thoroughly that miracles break through.

In the final analysis, however, the explanation for this kind of occasion counts less for me than a description which remains as faithful as possible to it. The bond of kinship I felt in that moment between soul and star is what matters. Bonds of kinship are ties of affection and love, and it seems to me that this occasion demonstrates a simple and extraordinary truth: love is the field which yokes together soul and nature, self and star. I do not mean to suggest, however, any image of love which would forget its dark shadows. After all, to truly love requires the recognition of loss, and death is love's eternal partner. The stars, too, are born in explosions of energies, and if they are, in some sense, made from gestures of love, then it is a love which has both moments of creation and destruction.

And yet, love is and remains the cosmic force which, I believe, is common to soul and nature; hence, I agree with the physicist Michio Kaku when he says that "The equations of physics are the poems of nature."[7] Or, I almost agree, because I would add that these equations are the love poems of nature. The gravitational forces of attraction which wed galaxies together, no less than the strong and weak forces of attraction which respectively guard the fidelity of the nucleus and hold electrons in their orbits, are cosmic expressions of the bonds of love at the heart of matter. The soul participates in that same ocean of eros, and that is what grief dips into when it breaks the shells of isolation which harden the heart against the risks of love.

When the candlelight faded and the starry night sky flooded my room, the boundary between me and the world also faded. I felt restored to an intimacy which I once knew but had forgotten, and I felt embraced by that larger destiny of kinship between soul and star.

So, the starry night sky remains for me that wide expanse which receives my grief and, via a miracle, transforms it into love. Under that canopy, I have felt released from my sorrow, freed from my grief and the long, slow winter of mourning. I have felt as if I am a small step closer to home, closer to that destiny which launched my soul into this world and now awaits my return.

> When a baby is taken from a wet nurse
> it easily forgets her
> and starts eating solid food.
>
> Seeds feed awhile on ground
> then lift up into the sun.
>
> So you should taste the filtered light
> and work your way toward wisdom
> with no personal covering.
>
> That's how you came here, like a star
> without a name. Move across the night sky
> with those anonymous lights.[8]

NIGHT

My Xhosa companion and I had been traveling a twisting, bumpy nonroad which snaked its way between villages in the Transkei, one of those black homelands which the South African government had created under its system of apartheid. I had gone with my Xhosa companion to his home village, and, having met his sisters and participated in a wedding feast attended by two villages, we were driving back to Grahamstown.

The night was completely dark, except for the stars and their light, a darkness made palpable by the absence of any city lights. In this section of the Transkei there were no towns and nothing of the imprint of a Western technological society. There was only our car on this meandering nonroad which to me seemed unmarked and without any sense of direction. But my companion had grown up in this place and he guided our vehicle with a sureness which left me in peaceful repose. Except for the sound of the engine, the night was still, its quiet an even match for the thick darkness which surrounded us. I grew tired, and in time I fell asleep.

It was the absence of motion, I think, which awakened me. The night had grown chilly, and when I awoke it seemed quite late. Still half in dream, I wondered why we had stopped, and suddenly I realized that my Xhosa companion was gone. The door on his side of the car was closed; through the window I could see that he was nowhere in sight. I left the car, but something in me resisted the temptation to call out his name. Maybe it was the deep darkness, the canopy of shining stars and the quiet stillness of the night which kept me silent. Whatever it was, I felt drawn into the night and did not want to disturb it.

I walked perhaps fifty feet from the car and saw a dim light far on the horizon. Compared to the light of the stars it seemed feeble. I could not judge how distant it was or even what was there. Was it the headlight of another car or the glow of a fire? No, neither of these seemed right, for the light was still, not accompanied by any sense of movement. In the midst of all this darkness, I wondered if it was a lamp in a window of a house, a place of human habitation and perhaps of welcome for someone like myself who was alone and lost. But even if it were what I imagined, I knew that it was too far away, and that it did not beckon me to travel toward it. At that moment I stopped walking, and standing perfectly still I let myself be enveloped by the night.

The night sky held no moon but the stars, silver lights, dots of radiance, blanketed it, contrasting sharply with the thick blackness of the landscape. Their presence added an expanse to the landscape, enlarged it, and even deepened its blackness. In all that emptiness, I began to feel more than alone. It was as if I was shrinking in size, becoming a speck within all this vast open space.

At the same time, however, and in a way which makes no logical sense, I felt something within me grow beyond the boundaries of my embodied self. Simultaneously as my body felt itself shrinking, something other, something like a wind, a spirit, the soul of myself was expanding. The experience was intensely erotic, like an orgasmic release, and a part of me knew without any doubt that if I did not do something to break the spell I would disappear, become one with all the dark empty openness and become as large as the field of stars. But I did not want this feeling, so deeply pleasurable, to end, and besides it felt as if the moment for me to act had passed. I was in a state of surrender, cleansed of myself, emptied of who I was, embraced by the open cosmos in this faraway place of the Transkei, which earlier I had entered as a stranger. At the climax of the experience, the moment when death seemed a bride, I heard in the dark openness a name. The voice which spoke it was soft and feminine in tone. It whispered the name of my wife, Janet. Her name came from the vast, open, starry darkness itself, calling me, welcoming me, enclosing me within a lover's embrace. In that moment, I and the stars were one. In that moment, I passed beyond death through love into the stars.

How long that moment lasted I cannot say. I can say only that the part of me which had merged with the cosmos was called back to itself by the sound of my companion's voice, who had come looking for me. With his voice the stars retreated into their distance, the landscape became again only a dark night, and all that which, for a while, I had become, was in a torrent funneled back into the smaller "I" of my body. Although I never told my companion, I could swear that the transition of myself from star back into an embodied being was accompanied by a sound that had the force of a strong wind. When we continued our journey I was relieved to be in the car, next to my companion, flesh alongside flesh, and sad, knowing that I had glimpsed and left behind a cosmic experience of love. Only recently have I discovered that, according to an ancient Egyptian death ritual, one becomes a star at the end of one's life, "rotating in heaven with the never-setting circumpolar stars." [9]

So many small deaths mark our lives, so many moments occur when we are offered a foretaste of final parting. 'Night' is one of these little deaths. After Janet died 'Night' has often returned, and in its ambience I always feel its kinship with her actual death. That moment of 'Night' was also a death. I felt it then. Now on occasion that moment and her actual death reverberate. They belong together not only because of the mood of grief and loss which they share, but also because of the way in which 'Night', like my grief, opens a path beyond grief to the stars. The soul holds on to 'Night' and offers it to me again after

Janet's death, because that moment already contained the seed of my path into and out of grief. Time, we are told, heals all wounds. In the time of the soul, the wound itself is the path of healing.

I must confess, however, that when I tell this story of 'Night,' I am sometimes told that it has no place in the process of my grief, because it, and others like it which I tell, happened before Janet died. But how can I refuse to accept my experience of grief and its unfolding for the sake of some idea of how it should be? I cannot refuse. I can only remain as faithful as I can to the experience as it has unfolded, and in that fidelity there are these occasions when the line of time dissolves and moments gather together in the soul's deep and different rhythms.

In the story of the leopard I spoke of moments in time in terms of their archetypal timeless quality. Grief and loss, love and death, have an archetypal depth to them, and in these depths moments in time lose their local character. 'Night' crosses a boundary and communicates with the awful moment of Janet's death. The differences between then and now, between before and after, are erased.

I often find it odd that we are more willing to entertain this strange notion of time when we read about the quantum effect in physics. This effect describes how two events which are separated in space and time nevertheless influence other across these boundaries. For this reason, physics claims that events in the quantum field have a non-local character. Perhaps we can entertain this notion from physics easier than we accept it as part of the soul's way of being in time, because it remains an idea and does not have to be felt as an actual experience. But it seems to me that the soul lives this way, that its time has a natural non-local quality, and that we know this in the depths of our souls before the mind of physics knows it. I think that the soul has knowledge that only later does the mind come to know.

When I think back now to those early moments of grief, to those moments when my wife's death was still a terror too brutal to remember, I cannot imagine that I would ever have arrived at this place where I can occasionally hear the whisper of a destiny which calls me beyond my sorrow. But in the night, when the world is silent and at rest, the stars do seem like a vocation, and I can hear the melody of their conversations. I have no way to prove what I am saying, but this melody is a song of love which waters my soul. Long ago, the Persian poet Rumi responded in "A Night for Departure" in human words to this song of the stars:

> Oh lovers, lovers it is time
> to set out from the world.
> I hear a drum in my soul's ear
> coming from the depths of the stars.[10]

Perhaps the most curious aspect of grief is its capacity to make us into better lovers by opening the heart to those bonds of kinship between the soul and the cosmos. But I must confess that if this is so, then it is a miracle beyond our own feeble capacity either to produce or truly understand. Miracles happen. Moments of grace and redemption do occur. In these moments, I have always been only a witness, grateful for the invitation to be present to the moment.

DOME, MOON, AND STAR

It was already quite late and the square in front of Saint Peter's Church in Rome, thronged with camera laden tourists only hours ago, was empty. There was a slight chill in the early April air which made the Roman night colder than we had expected. That slight chill quickened our pace as we crossed the square, but it was not so cold that I failed to notice the wonderful alignment of Saint Peter's dome, moon, and single star in the night sky.

Saint Peter's is surely a place to dream. Earlier in the day we were overwhelmed by its history and awed by the splendor of this magnificent building. Now, having returned at night, even if only to cross the square on our way back to our hotel, we were prepared to be awed and overwhelmed again. But the square was different. Something had changed. A slight shift, almost imperceptible, had altered the landscape. A crescent moon, just a thin slice, hung directly above the dome, and just above one of the moon's horns, delicately balanced like a jewel, rested a silver star. Dome, moon, and star were like an arrow pointing in the direction from earth to the sky.

I cannot say why this alignment halted my steps, causing me to alert my companion to this strange geometry. I know there was a sense of beauty in this arrangement, a stark, naked kind of beauty, quite appealing in its simplicity. The perfect precision of the line connecting dome, moon, and star was magical, and in the elegance of this form everything else in the landscape was eclipsed. But as I continued to stare at this alignment, I sensed that its mathematical harmony was also a song and that in this song, in the precision and direction of that line from dome through moon to star, there was a simple refrain: the cosmos is older than we, and in spite of our magnificent achievements, we are witnessed and placed by forces and powers greater than ourselves. For a moment the architectural splendor of the dome was overshadowed by the fragile beauty of that moon crowned on one of its horns with the shining jewel of a star.

The dome of Saint Peters Church is one of the splendors of the world. It incarnates in stone one of the great dreams of the human soul: its dream of the eternal sense of spirit and of light in the realm of the divine. But on this night I realized that our dreams are truly enfolded by the larger dreams of the cosmos. So, too, are our loves and sorrows. I imagine now that, in fact, our labors and our loves, like this dome as a labor of love, are the ways in which the larger dreams of the cosmos are realized. We truly are "such stuff, as dreams are made on."[11]

LOVE, DEATH, AND HOMECOMING ~

In the early moments of grief, I was a ghost in the world, and my sense of isolation was almost total. The truth, however, is that the process of grieving and the long, slow winter of mourning dissolved that separateness in unexpected ways. After the winter passes, after the ice around the heart, broken in grief, has melted, a new sense of intimacy with the world appears, an intimacy whose boundaries explode the usual parameters not only of space but also of time. In these moments, I have felt myself attached to others with a compassion which I have not known before and drawn, too, beyond myself to the green brilliance of the world, to the cat with a smile of recognition for me, to the wave and the wind, and to the starry night sky and the light.

LIGHT, TIME, HOME

Venasque, a small village in Provence, Southern France, the valley of the Luberon, on a Sunday afternoon. About four years after my wife's death I was in this village overlooking the valley, the mountains in the distance. No one else was present. Only the light and the smell of the air. Sitting on a bench in the courtyard of a church, now closed, now cold and silent, the dampness of its

*stones contrasting so sharply with the warmth of the sun,
I slipped into that place between waking and dreaming,
into reverie where some small treasure, a tiny gift of the
soul, a seed of remembrance, always waits.*

*In this state of reverie, freed of the usual weight of
personal memory, I was like a cloud drifting in a blue sky
on a lazy summer day, an atom of wispy boundlessness, a
speck of airy nothingness. The color of the light against
the distant mountains was a sweet melody, almost like a
lullaby, a tone so soothing that I began to feel myself
dissolving into its rhythms, becoming the light itself. And
then, out of this sensuous field, heard, like a whisper, as
if said in passing, perhaps to some others, invisible and
unseen, those who perhaps had been there before or those
who were yet to come, I heard these words: "C'est la
totalitie de la vie et un absence complet" —this moment
is the totality of life, everything and nothing, a fullness
and an emptiness. I recall thinking how odd and yet
appropriate that in this French landscape the voice spoke
in its mother tongue.*

*I was in Venasque on a warm Sunday afternoon,
but I was elsewhere too, in the place of my boyhood, in
Brooklyn of long ago. In this moment, they were one and
the same, each a palimpsest of the other, confused,
blended, mixed, woven together, a resonant harmony of
places and times. It was Venasque of that day, that Sunday
afternoon, and Brooklyn of that other day, of older,
archaic Sunday afternoons, of moments that I loved for
their pace and rhythm, and for the light which promised
eternity. It was Venasque now and Brooklyn then, their
separation in time erased, the essence of all Sunday*

afternoons, the archetype of that temporal moment, its stillness and tranquillity, a smell, a quality of air, a sound in the distance, a color of light. It was two moments drawn together by a love forgotten by me, but remembered in the cells of my body and encoded in the soul, patient and waiting for just this moment to be released by the light.

Venasque-Brooklyn! I felt the elusive sense of home, how home has always been a phantom presence, lingering there just beyond my reach, shimmering over there just beyond the grasp of my outstretched hand, a haunting that has always filled me with a longing as eternal as that brief moment between two heartbeats, when nothing can be done, when nothing can be either said or thought to contain the moment, to hold onto it, when I can be only still and silent, and simply wait, and give thanks.

This moment of light was Venasque and it was Brooklyn, a singular moment, one moment, everything and nothing. It was Venasque, and it was Brooklyn, a fissure in the fabric of time, when the sequential linearity of time breaks down and two moments find their kinship in the presence of a witness. I felt as I were in the presence of a pure drop of time and that it was a white pearl, a shimmering diamond, a radiant crystal, a glowing star. One moment, complete in itself, prelude to nothing else; this moment, a totality in itself, passage to nowhere.

In Venasque on that Sunday afternoon I understood that grief restores the time of the soul, plunges us into its rhythms, where moments are gathered together because of their affinity for each other. These moments are like the air we breathe: we are in their time, their time is not in us. I know now, therefore, that I do not carry that place and its moment of long ago within me as a memory. Rather, it carries me and is always around me, just as Venasque was present then so long ago in Brooklyn. On those warm Sunday afternoons of long ago, I was already being drawn to Venasque, for how else to account for the appeal of the light of those moments if they were not already etched as a destiny of my soul. I am not saying that I traveled to France because of my wife's death or that somehow her death was the cause of my journey. No! I am saying only that, in a way I do not understand, the light of Venasque and Brooklyn are stitched into the same fabric of my life which includes my wife's death. In ways I will never understand, these moments belong together.

The painter Paul Cezanne knew this secret of light, that it carried in itself those occasions wedded together in a kinship outside the normal parameters of space and time. Indeed, for Cezanne a moment of light was a container for all moments of time, which is why he once said that all he ever wanted to do was to paint one moment of the world's being. He knew that if he could capture just one moment, he would capture the totality of all creation. The physicist too knows this secret of light and time as moments of kinship. As I said earlier, in its principle of nonlocality of events, physics attends to events which are not circumscribed to particular regions of time or space and which are, therefore, in instantaneous communication with each other. I must confess that I laugh now when I think that grief has led me to this same insight, where Venasque and Brooklyn were in instantaneous relation. What is the kinship here between the mind of physics and the soul of grief?

Of course, I have no answer to this question, but I do raise it in order to say that the soul of grief adds something to this notion of nonlocality. I believe that it adds the recognition that love is the magnet which draws and holds together moments and places otherwise separate in time and space. If grief has enlarged me—and it has—then it is because grief has dissolved the specificity of events and places and released their light. Venasque and Brooklyn are radiations of light, moods, vibrations of energy dispersed throughout the cosmos, waiting, longing, desiring each other, joining, coupling, like two lovers, in that one instant of time, and then gone, departed, like a death between lovers, dispersed again into the wide, throbbing ribbon of cosmic energy, perhaps for a thousand years or more, until the next moment when a hunger for kinship beyond measure draws them together again for another epiphany.

In April 1923, the poet Rilke wrote a letter to his wife, marveling at how an experience in Russia in 1899 had come to figure in one of the sonnets in *Sonnets to Orpheus*, written in 1922. In sonnet twenty he asks what he should dedicate to Orpheus, that figure of myth whose songs were so sweet that they even persuaded the Gods to release his beloved bride, Eurydice, from the bonds of death. Rilke's response is that experience of a spring evening in 1899 in Russia when, traveling with Lou Andreas Salome, he saw a white horse gallop toward them. A fleeting moment, but, for him, the very best tribute to Orpheus, whose songs were as sweet and as elusive as the breeze. A small moment, nothing of great import really, and yet, for Rilke, seemingly a miracle. It led him to wonder what is time?, what is the present? "Isn't it lovely," he wrote to his wife April 1923, "that the white horse I 'experienced' with Lou on a meadow in Russia in 1899 or 1900, bounded through my heart again? That after all nothing is lost!"[12]

DANCING WITH A GHOST

It was always in the night and always after a long day of teaching, where I was in the company of so many people. I would return to my office and a wave of loneliness would wash over me. On these occasions within the first year of my wife's death, I was acutely reminded of the harsh permanence of her absence. This harsh quality was often emphasized by the contrast between this complete and total absence and those other times when I knew I would see her again after a trip which either she or I had taken. Now there was nothing to look forward to, no day or time when I could telephone, no happy expectation of a letter, no sweet fantasy of an airport reunion. Nothing! Only this void, this black hole, this dark emptiness.

On these occasions, music was my only solace. Sitting in the darkness of my office one evening, I heard on the radio the old English melody, "Greensleeves." This was not a melody that either my wife or I had ever considered to be one of our songs, but on this occasion I was quite moved by it. Tears came to my eyes, and initially I remembered my father, who had died some ten years earlier. I heard in the melody something of his world, something ancient and slow, a world which belonged to the far shores of a European culture from where he had emigrated when he was a small boy. And then, the quality of the moment shifted, and my wife was in the room. As if a curtain had parted, she emerged from behind my father's world into this moment. The spaces and times of all three moments were now blended and confused with each other. The differences among these spaces and times had collapsed into a field of kinship among them.

She had come to dance with me. We moved slowly in time to the haunting rhythms of "Greensleeves." I felt her presence so intensely that while the song played she was no longer gone. But the melody ended, and as it did she began to fade. She "said" thanks, and she was gone. I smiled, and I cried because I knew she loved to dance.

For many months after this occasion, I tried to repeat this dance. I bought a tape of "Greensleeves," and in the seclusion of my office and the darkness of the night, I would play it. But she came back to dance only on very rare occasions. After a while I stopped, because I knew that I was not the creator of these moments, that they were not subject to my will or control.

"That after all nothing is lost!"[13] I know now that Rilke's insight is true, that for the soul nothing is lost. My wife is dead, and yet she lives. In her earthly form of flesh and bone and blood, in her presence as a smile and a word spoken in love, she is gone, forever. That cold, hard fact is the bitterness of grief, which always remains. But there are those moments, especially under the stars, when the day is surrendering into night, that she glides through my heart again. These moments are the other, sweeter taste of grief. And, again, although I am not the author of these moments, I can at least prepare the occasion and make myself ready for them when, and if, they come.

PREPARING THE GROUND

Ocracoke is a small island, part of the Outer Banks off the coast of North Carolina. For one of my sabbaticals, Janet and I had rented a house on the island and for nearly six months we lived there, becoming part of its community, learning to track the path of storms by map and radio, and most of all enjoying those occasions when we would make the twelve-mile journey to the ferry to cross to the mainland, and then travel the forty or so miles through small towns on the way to Kitty Hawk for weekly supplies.

It was a lovely time for us, long lazy mornings of

writing or reading and afternoons of beach walking or trail hiking in one of the island's protected nature reserves. Janet was a photographer, and she spent many hours recording the unique treasures of the island: the lighthouse, the two cemeteries, the abandoned houses, and the twisting roads. We even planned a joint project of photos and text about roads and journeys, intrigued by the image of what lay beyond the next, inviting bend in a road. We were happy there.

As the time to leave drew near, we both realized that this place would always matter to us, and so we made a pact. On one of the trails in the nature reserve, we pledged to return to this island when either one of us had died. On this island we would find each other again, because this place had held us and would do so even beyond death. I remember thinking in that moment that Janet would be the one to make this sad journey, and I wished I could spare her from it. I could not even imagine it the other way, perhaps because I was too afraid to imagine her death and the grief which would follow. To die before her would spare me that pain. The fear of losing the one I loved made me selfish in this way.

But she did die first, and it was I who had to make this journey. I put it off as long as I could, but finally two years after her death there came a moment when it felt right to return. I asked Veronica to accompany me, because I wanted to introduce her to Janet, and it seemed to me that this was the proper way to do it. Veronica was a sensitive woman who respected my grief and the ways in which it often made me unavailable for our relationship. We were learning to love each other, doing that hard work of love, and I felt I could not return to this island to keep my promise without letting Janet know of her.

We spent several days on the island, and at first I tried to be a cheerful tourist in search of his memories. We cycled, walked, and visited places which held more or less pleasant memories for me. But I knew in my heart that I was avoiding the moment which had brought me back, and I knew that I would have to prepare myself for it.

I travelled the twelve mile road to the ferry, crossed to the mainland, and drove through those small towns on the way to Kitty Hawk. I went alone, in search of the mood of my feelings, trying to get to the sadness below the fear of experiencing my loss again. When I returned in the evening, I was not at all convinced I had succeeded. I felt estranged, from myself, from Veronica, from this island. I was angry, which was easier than being afraid.

When the morning came, I knew that I had to walk those trails again in the nature reserve. Janet was waiting for me there all this time, and somewhere deep within me I knew that. I had avoided this one place for the entire week, and now it was time to keep my promise. Veronica came with me, and we walked the trail in silence. I was listening for something, for some clue about where to stop and linger, but I did not know how I would recognize it. And then, at a bend in the trail, I found the place.

Beneath an ancient tree, I buried our wedding rings, and made a small ceremony of dedication. On this spot, I made a place to hold the symbols of our love, and I hoped that this ceremony of dedication would establish a field which one day, perhaps, would embrace others.

When we left the trail, I imagined that at some other place in time, two lovers would experience a moment which they would not quite understand, but whose force would unite them in kinship with our moment of love.

ENDINGS AND BEGINNINGS ~

Today, as I write these words, I am living in a house which is just below the house of my dear friend, Charles, the one who did for me that nearly impossible task of removing Janet's rings in the hospital, just moments after she died. It was to his house that I went immediately after the hospital when Janet had died. Now about seven years since that day I am married again, and, with my wife Veronica, doing the work of loving as we make a new home. To love again, especially after loss, and to be loved, is a miracle.

This very morning, as I write these final words, Charles waves to me as I drink my coffee and calls my name in greeting. In the same moment, Veronica enters the patio and waves in greeting to Charles. That room in his house where my life ended nearly seven years ago is now the place from which he calls my name, and it seems to me that his greeting is the mark of a new beginning. Love and death, endings and beginnings, are commingled here, and I am certain that these places and times share that kinship which characterizes the rhythms of the soul.

I am a lucky man. I have been visited in the darkest moments of my grief by grace, and it is because of that, that otherwise unnameable wisdom and beauty of the soul, and not because of my own will, that I am here to tell this story. Shortly after Janet died, I dreamed that I went to Charles' house and knocked on his front door. A party was in progress, and I hesitated to enter. But he welcomed me, and when I crossed the threshold I saw Janet, dressed in a radiant garment of green. She was alive, and I was dead. Now, by virtue of that grace, I am alive again. The final word can be only one of thanks.

REFERENCES

PART ONE

Chapter 1:

1. Larry Dossey. "Angels: The Missing Link," In *A Gathering of Angels,* edited by Robert Sardello (Dallas, Texas: The Dallas Institute Publications, 1990), p. 45.
2. *Ibid.*, p.48.
3. Gaston Bachelard, *The Poetics of Reverie,* trans. Daniel Russell (New York: The Orion Press, 1969), p. 72.

PART TWO

Chapter 2:

1. William Shakespeare, *The Tempest,* Act IV, Scene 1, lines 173–174. In *The New Folger Library Shakespeare* (New York: Washington Square Press, 1974).
2. The quote actually reads: "you are dust, and to dust you shall return." *Genesis,* 3:19. In *The Holy Bible, New Revised Standard Version* (New York: Oxford University Press, 1989), p. 4.
3. Gaston Bachelard, *The Poetics of Reverie*, trans. Daniel Russell (New York: The Orion Press, 1969), p. 23.
4. Rainer Maria Rilke, *Duino Elegies,* trans. J. B. Leishman and Stephen Spender (New York: W. W. Norton and Company, 1939), pp.25–27.
5. Bachelard, *The Poetics of Reverie*, p. 187.
6. The full etymologies can be found in Ernest Klein, *A Comprehensive Etymological Dictionary of the English Language* (Amsterdam, London, New York: Elsevier Publishing Company, 1971).
7. Bachelard, *The Poetics of Reverie*, p. 6.
8. Rilke, *Duino Elegies*, p. 21.
9. Henri Bosco, *L'antiquaire* (Paris: Gallimard 1979), p. 121.
10. Alain Bosquet, *Premier Testament* (Paris: Gallimard 1957), p. 52.
11. Bachelard, *The Poetics of Reverie,* pp. 15, 8, 73.
12. E. E. Cummings, "is 5," in *E. E. Cummings Complete Poems 1904-1962,* edited by George J. Firmage (New York: Liveright Publishing Corporation, 1994), p. 291.
13. *Ibid.*, p. 262
14. I have paraphrased here the lines of the first stanza. See Rainer Maria Rilke, *Sonnets to Orpheus,* trans. M. D. Herter Norton (New York: W. W. Norton and Company, 1962), p. 25.
15. Pierre Albert-Birot, *Les Memoires d'Adam* (Paris: Editions Balzac,1943), p. 126.
16. Rainer Maria Rilke, *Duino Elegies,* p. 79.

Chapter 3:

1. William Anderson, *Green Man: The Archetype of Our Oneness with the Earth* (London and San Francisco: Harper Collins, 1990), p. 14.
2. *Ibid.*
3. *Ibid.*, p. 91.
4. Dylan Thomas, "The Force that Throught the Green Fuse Drives the Flower," in *The Poems of Dylan Thomas,* edited with an introduction by Daniel Jones (New York: New Directions, 1971), p. 77.
5. Anderson, *Green Man*, p. 157.
6. Heinrich Heine in Gaston Bachelard, *The Poetics of Reverie*, trans. Daniel Russell (New York: The Orion Press, 1969), p. 33.
7. *Ibid.*
8. Rainer Maria Rilke, *Selected Poems of Rainer Maria Rilke*, edited by Robert Bly (New York: Harper and Row, 1981), p. 11.
9. Rumi, *Mathnawi*, unpublished translation by Coleman Barks, personal communication.
10. Rainer Maria Rilke, *Selected Poems of Rainer Maria Rilke*, p. 67.
11. Bachelard, *The Poetics of Reverie*, p. 203.
12. Rainer Marie Rilke, *Sonnets to Orpheus*, trans. M. D. Herter Norton (New York: W. W. Norton and Company, 1962), pp. 133-34.
13. Itzhak Bentov, *Stalking the Wild Pendulum* (New York: E. P. Dutton, 1977), p. 126.
14. *Ibid.*, p. 128.

Chapter 4:

1. Rainer Maria Rilke, *Duino Elegies,* trans. J. B. Leishman and Stephen Spender (New York: WW. Norton and Company, 1939), p. 21.
2. *Ibid.*, pp. 69–71.
3. Robert D. Romanyshyn, *Technology as Symptom and Dream* (London, New York: Routledge, 1989).
4. Rilke, *Duino Elegies*, p. 77.
5. Noel Cobb, "Hymn to the Star." In *Sphinx 7: A Journal for Archetypal Psychology and the Arts* (London: The London Convivium, 1996), p. 17.
6. Robert Romanyshyn, "So Fierce Its Streaming Beauty, So Terrible Its Averted Gaze: On Once Encountering an Angel," In *A Gathering of Angels*, edited by Robert Sardello (Dallas: The Dallas Institute Publications, 1990), pp. 16–21.
7. Rilke, *Duino Elegies*, p. 29.
8. Blaise Pascal, *Pensees and Other Writings,* trans. Honor Levi, with Introduction and Notes by Anthony Levi (New York: Oxford University Press, 1995), p. 158.
9. Emily Dickinson, *Final Harvest: Emily Dickinson's Poems,* Edited and Introduction by Thomas H. Johnson (Boston: Little, Brown and Company, 1961), p. 248.

10. H. C. Moolenburgh, *A Handbook of Angels*, trans. Amina Marix-Evans (Great Britain: The C. W. Daniel Company Limited, 1984), p. 249.
11. Rilke, *Duino Elegies*, p. 31.
12. Rainer Maria Rilke, *Sonnets to Orpheus*, trans. M. D. Herter Norton (New York: WW. Norton and Company, 1962), p. 135.
13. Robert D. Romanyshyn, "The Orphan and the Angel: In Defense of Melancholy," In *Psychological Perspectives*, Fall-Winter, 1995, No. 32 (Los Angeles: C. G. Jung Institute), p. 104.
14. Rilke, *Duino Elegies*, p. 75.

PART THREE

Chapter 5:

1. Rainer Maria Rilke, *Sonnets to Orpheus*, trans. M. D. Herter Norton (New York: WW. Norton and Company, 1962), p. 31.
2. *Ibid.*, p. 29.
3. *Ibid.*, p. 133.
4. *Ibid.*, p. 33.
5. *Ibid.*, p. 27.
6. Rainer Maria Rilke, *Duino Elegies*, trans. J. B. Leishman and Stephen Spender (New York: W. W. Norton and Company, 1939), p. 21.
7. Gaston Bachelard, *The Poetics of Reverie*, trans. Daniel Russell (New York: The Orion Press, 1969), p. 112.
8. Walt Whitman, *Walt Whitman: The Complete Poems* , edited by Francis Murphy (New York: Penguin Books, 1986), p. 463.
9. Bachelard, *The Poetics of Reverie*, p. 188.
10. Rabindranath Tagore, *Fireflies* (New York: MacMillian, 1935), p. 205.
11. Emily Dickinson, *The Poems of Emily Dickinson*, edited by Martha Dickinson Branchi and Alfred Lette Hampson (Boston: Little, Brown and Company, 1932), p.17.

Chapter 6:

1. Gaston Bachelard, *The Poetics of Reverie*, trans. Daniel Russell (New York: The Orion Press, 1969), p. 65.
2. Stephen Levine, *Who Dies? An Investigation of Conscious Living and Conscious Dying* (New York: Anchor Books, 1982), p. 74.
3. Sigmund Freud, "Mourning and Melancholia," In *The Standard Edition of the Complete Psychological Works of Sigmund Freud*, trans. James Strachey in collaboration with Anna Freud, Vol. 14 (London: The Hogarth Press, 1957) pp. 237–258.
4. Robert D. Romanyshyn, *Technology as Symptom and Dream* (London, New York: Routledge, 1989).
5. Kathleen Raine, *Autobiographies* (London: Skoob Books, 1991), p. 3.

6. Bachelard, *The Poetics of Reverie.* p. 99.

7. Jean Follain, *Territoires* (Paris: Gallimard 1953) p. 30.

8. Rainer Maria Rilke, *Duino Elegies.* trans. J. B. Leishman and Stephen Spender (New York: W. W. Norton and Company, 1939), p. 77.

9. Romanyshyn, *Technology as Symptom and Dream*, pp. 2–3.

10. Robert D. Romanyshyn, "Technology and Homecoming: Southern Africa As Landscape of the Soul," In *Modern South Africa in Search of a Soul*, edited by Graham Saayman (Boston: Sigo Press, 1990), pp. 69–71.

11. I wrote this poem while on an extended visit to South Africa before my wife died. Looking back, I remember how much I felt our separation as a kind of death. But again, I never thought that she would actually one day be gone. I always thought we had time.

12. As quoted by Georges Charbonnier, *Le monologue de peintre* (Paris: R. Juilliard, 1959-60), p. 143.

13. Bachelard, *The Poetics of Reverie*, p. 80.

Chapter 7:

1. Rainer Maria Rilke, *Duino Elegies*, trans. J. B. Leishman and Stephen Spender (New York: W. W. Norton and Company, 1939), p. 129.

2. Marie-Louise von Franz, *Projection and Recollection in Jungian Psychology*, trans. William H. Kennedy (La Salle and London: Open Court, 1980), p. 140.

3. Rainer Maria Rilke, *Letters To a Young Poet*, trans. M. D. Herter Norton (New York: W. W. Norton and Company, 1934), p. 54.

4. Robert D. Romanyshyn, *Technology as Symptom and Dream* (London, New York: Routledge, 1989).

5. Carl Jung,"Synchronicity: An Acausal Connecting Principle,"In *Collected Works, Vol.8* (Princeton: Princeton University Press, 1952/1969), pp. 417–531.

6. Marie-Louise von Franz, *Psyche and Matter* (Boston: Shambhala Publications, 1992), p. 162.

7. Michio Kaku, *Hyperspace* (New York: Oxford University Press, 1994), p. 130.

8. Rumi, "A Star Without a Name," In *Say I Am You*, trans. John Moyne and Coleman Barks (Athens, GA: Maypop, 1994), p. 59.

9. Von Franz, *Psyche and Matter*, p. 60, note 10.

10. Rumi, *Love Is a Stranger*, trans. Kabir Edmund Helminski (Putney, VT: Threshold Books, 1993), p. 77.

11. William Shakespeare, *The Tempest*, Act IV, Scene 1, Lines 173–174. In *The New Folger Library Shakespeare* (New York: Washington Square Press, 1974).

12. Rainer Maria Rilke, *Sonnets to Orpheus*, trans. M. D. Herter Norton (New York: W. W. Norton and Company, 1962), p. 150.

13. *Ibid.*

BIBLIOGRAPHY

Albert-Birot, Pierre. *Les memoires d'Adam*. Paris: Editions Balzac, 1943.

Alighieri, Dante. *The Divine Comedy*, translated with an introduction and notes by H. R. Huse. New York: Harcourt, Brace, Jovanovich, 1954.

Anderson, William. *Green Man: The Archetype of Our Oneness with the Earth*. London and San Francisco: Harper Collins, 1990.

Bachelard, Gaston. *The Poetics of Reverie*, translated by Daniel Russell. New York: The Orion Press, 1969.

Bentou, Itzhak. *Stalking the Wild Pendulum*. New York: E.P. Dutton, 1977.

Bosco, Henri. *L'antiquaire*. Paris: Gallimard, 1979.

Bosquet, Alain. *Premiere testament*. Paris: Gallimard, 1957.

Charbonnier, Georges. *Le monologue de peintre*. Paris: R. Julliard, 1959-60.

Cobb, Noel. *Sphinx 7: A Journal for Archetypal Psychology and the Arts*. London: The London Convivium, 1996.

Cummings, E. E. *E.E. Cummings Complete Poems 1904-1962,* edited by Georges J. Firmage. New York: Liveright Publishing Corporation, 1994.

Dickinson, Emily. *The Poems of Emily Dickinson*, edited by Martha Dickinson Branchi and Alfred Lette Hampson. Boston: Little, Brown and Company, 1932.

———. *Final Harvest: Emily Dickinson's Poems,* edited and introduction by Thomas H. Johnson. Boston: Little, Brown and Company, 1961.

Dossey, Larry. "Angels: The Missing Link," in *A Gathering of Angels*, edited by Robert Sardello. Dallas, Texas: The Dallas Institute Publications, 1990.

Follain, Jean. *Territoires*. Paris: Gallimard, 1953.

Fox, Matthew and Ruppert Sheldrake. *The Physics of Angels*. San Francisco: Harper Collins, 1996.

Freud, Sigmund. "Mourning and Melancholia," in *The Standard Edition of the Complete Psychological Works of Sigmund Freud*, translated by James Strachey in collaboration with Anna Freud, Vol. 14. London: The Hogarth Press, 1957.

Genesis, in The Holy Bible, New Revised Standard Version. New York: Oxford University Press, 1989.

Jung, Carl. "Synchronicity: An Acausal Connecting Principle," in *The Structure and Dynamics of the Psyche*, translated by R. F. C. Hull, Collected Works, Vol. 8. Princeton: Princeton University Press, 1952.

Kaku, Michio. *Hyperspace*. New York: Oxford University Press, 1994.

Klein, Ernest. *A Comprehensive Etymological Dictionary of the English Language*. Amsterdam, London, New York: Elsevier Publishing Company, 1971.

Levine, Stephen. *Who Dies? An Investigation of Conscious Living and Conscious Dying*. New York: Anchor Books, 1982.

Moolenburgh, H. C. *A Handbook of Angels,* translated by Amina Marix-Evans. Great Britain: The C. W. Daniel Company Limited, 1984.

Neruda, Pablo. *The Book of Questions*, translated by William O'Daly. Port Townsend: Copper Canyon Press, 1991.

Pascal, Blaise. *Pensees and Other Writings*, translated by Honor Levi with an Introduction and notes by Anthony Levi. New York: Oxford University Press, 1995.

Raine, Kathleen. *Autobiographies*. London: Skoob Books, 1991.

Rilke, Rainer Maria. *Letters to a Young Poet*, translated by M. D. Herter Norton. New York: W. W. Norton and Company, 1939.

———. *Duino Elegies*, translated by J. B. Leishman and Stephen Spender. New York: W. W. Norton and Company, 1939.

———. *Sonnets to Orpheus*, translated by M. D. Herter Norton. New York: W. W. Norton and Company, 1962.

———. *Selected Poems of Rainer Maria Rilke*, edited by Robert Bly. New York: Harper and Row, 1981.

Romanyshyn, Robert D. *Technology as Symptom and Dream*. London, New York: Routledge,1989.

———. "So Fierce Its Streaming Beauty, So Terrible Its Averted Gaze," in *A Gathering of Angels*, edited by Robert Sardello. Dallas, Texas: The Dallas Institute Publications, 1990.

———. "Technology and Homecoming: Southern Africa As Landscape of the Soul", in *Modern South Africa in Search of a Soul*, edited by Graham Saayman. Boston: Sigo Press, 1990.

———. "The Orphan and the Angel: In Defense of Melancholy," in *Psychological Perspectives*, Fall-Winter, 1995, No. 32. Los Angeles: C. G. Jung Institute.

Rumi, Jalal Al-Din. *Mathnawi,* unpublished translation by Coleman Barks, personal communication.

———. *Love Is a Stranger*, trans. Kabir Edmund Helminski. Putney, Vt: Threshold Books, 1993.

———. *Say I Am You*, trans. John Moyne and Coleman Barks. Athens, GA: Maypop, 1994.

Shakespeare, William. *The Tempest, in The New Folger Library Shakespeare*. New York: Washington Square Press, 1974.

Tagore, Rabindranath. *Fireflies*. New York: MacMillian, 1935.

Thomas, Dylan. *The Poems of Dylan Thomas*, edited with an introduction by Daniel Jones. New York: New Directions, 1971.

Von Franz, Maria-Louise. *Projection and Recollection in Jungian Psychology*, translated by William H. Kennedy. La Salle and London: Open Court, 1980.

———. *Psyche and Matter*. Boston: Shambhala Publications, 1992.

Whitman, Walt. *Walt Whitman, The Complete Poems*, edited by Francis Murphy. New York: Penguin Books, 1986.